Arch

THE CITY OF

TO-MORROW

334 705

LP/sv

A LONDON SUBURB

The town spread out over an immense area.   Narrow "corridor" streets.   Back gardens that are lit
more than yards.

The City of To=morrow

AND ITS PLANNING

by LE CORBUSIER

*translated from the 8th French Edition
of* URBANISME *by*

FREDERICK ETCHELLS

LONDON
THE ARCHITECTURAL PRESS LTD

ISBN 0 85139 124 9 (paperback)
0 85139 125 7 (hardback)
This translation copyright © 1929
New material copyright © 1947 and 1971
by the Architectural Press Ltd
First published in England, 1929
Second edition, 1947
Third edition 1971
Reprinted 1977, 1978

Printed litho in Great Britain by Biddles Ltd, Guildford, Surrey

THIS BOOK WAS FIRST PUBLISHED in Paris in 1924, by Editions Crés, under the title *Urbanisme*. The first English edition was translated from the 8th French edition by Mr. Frederick Etchells and published by John Rodker in 1929 under the title *The City of Tomorrow*, but has long been out of print. The 1947 edition was an exact facsimile (slightly reduced in page size) of the first English edition, containing all the original illustrations chosen by M. Le Corbusier. This 1971 edition (reprinted in 1977) is likewise a facsimile of the 1929 edition.

CONTENTS

PREFACE TO THE 1947 EDITION

To my surprise the Architectural Press insists categorically on reprinting, in its English version, my book *Urbanisme*, which I wrote in 1924.

In this book there were brought together various articles on town planning which had appeared in *l'Esprit Nouveau*, an international review of contemporary activities, during the year which preceded the International Exhibition of Decorative Art, in Paris. We had been fighting for architecture, for town planning, and for the major arts, as against merely decorative art.

Vers Une Architecture[1] had already appeared in 1923. In it were grouped various articles from *l'Esprit Nouveau's* first year of publication (1920–1921), and it was received as a manifesto, and indeed seems still to be thought of as such to-day. Translations of it appeared in England, the United States, Russia, Mexico, Germany, and Japan.

The year 192., saw the appearance in *l'Esprit Nouveau* of the studies on the "Decorative Art of To-day", on "Town Planning", and finally on "Modern Painting", which formed the basis of three books published in 1925.[2]

There are no minor matters in art. There can, moreover, be no question of decorative art having a minor character and town planning a major one: there lies always the choice between pettiness and greatness every day of a man's life and in every action undertaken.

L'Art Decoratif d'Aujourd'hui, under this quite commonplace title, made its appeal to the modern conscience at a time pregnant with grandiose and dangerous activities.

La Peinture Moderne carried the discussion on into the mysteries of understanding and of creative work. The book gave for the first time a coherent account of that extraordinary event in the expression of plastic thought, the invention of Cubism.

---

[1] *Towards a New Architecture*, translated by Frederick Etchells, John Rodker 1927. Reprinted by the Architectural Press, 1946, reissued 1970.

[2] *Urbanisme, L'Art Decoratif d'Aujourd'hui, La Peinture Moderne*. Editions Crés et Cie.

Urbanisme, dating from 1924, is in a similar vein and follows the same line of thought. Twenty years have passed since then for the world, and twenty years have passed over my own shoulders. I myself have grown older by this stretch of time, but I am persuaded that the world itself has grown younger in its journey through the immensity of horror which has recently ended.

Now, are my contemporaries really aware that town planning is in actual fact a manifestation of resurgence? That it is the concrete expression of human needs, of human means, and of human intentions? These needs, these means, these intentions, are to-day clearly apparent to those who are capable of discernment and vision. And so town planning really becomes as it were, the mirror of authority and, it may be, the decisive act of governing. Is this, perhaps, to twist the meaning generally given to the expression "town planning"? Or is it, rather, a revolution which must be incorporated into the act of governing?

The people of England, in particular, seem to have understood these things, and are giving proof of their excellent gift for the close study of the reconstruction problems which face them.

What strikes me at all times, in the midst of the violent quarrels aroused by town planning, is the gulf, which grows greater, between those who hold this conception of town planning and the rest. A country as a whole, that is to say the mass of the people as well as their representatives, is not really conversant with the subject, with the immense range of its problems, with their bearing, or with the tremendous possibilities of its emancipating power. They are, on the contrary, entangled in the network of common custom which everywhere, in housing, in the streets and towns, and even in the use made of the land itself, has brought about a condition of uneasiness, to which one might well be tempted to impute the immense anguish of modern times: men are badly housed!

It is undoubtedly true to say that to think in terms of modern town planning is to open every door to harmony and happiness both in the homes and amongst the mass of mankind. And an appeal must be made to courage and enthusiasm. An obstinate desire to keep to traditional ways of town planning, now that their failure is shown to be complete, would be to turn our modern world back into the blind alley where it had gone astray.

The year 1945, by contrast with 1925, represents an enormous advance in town planning towards genuine solutions of the problem the world over. Twenty years press heavily on a society as intense as ours, and are productive. My book *Urbanisme*, dating from 1924, may serve as a preamble to present-day schemes, eliminating any appearance of casualness in these. *Urbanisme* opened the discussion (or one angle of it): this reprint will provide the historical background of a movement where some people imagine there is only improvisation.

Nevertheless, there will be found in the book certain aims and proposals which are certainly now out-of-date, and the reader will discover these for himself. Glancing at random through this book, which I have not re-read for twenty years, I notice, for instance, the scheme for a central underground railway station with its flat roof serving as an airport—a rather ingenuous solution which may cause a smile to-day, And yet, the latest requirements of modern town planning and of aviation may well tend to the retention of at least a part of my scheme: large air-liners should never land in closely built-up areas; some day only taxi airplanes, autogyros, or helicopters may be allowed to fly over our cities, and these could then suitably land on the roof-platform of this central station which had already been foreseen. The twenty years which have elapsed meanwhile have provided an opportunity for envisaging solutions of the problem more nearly akin to actual practice.

Further on, two pages of illustrations show a clear and definite scheme for the provision of vegetation in the city. A very modest solution of this problem as set forth at the date in question was the one which I called "Dwellings on the Cellular or Honey-comb System." These were elements on the scale of the *Palais Royal*, and a photograph of the *Palais Royal* gardens provided a very nearly foolproof reference. And yet we have my adversaries setting up the *Palais Royal* itself as a stick to beat me with! It is a characteristic test.

Elsewhere again in the book, I put forward my scheme for

cruciform skyscrapers. These vividly occupied my imagination and my plans over a period of ten years, and were to me as true radiators of light. Later, I saw that a quarter of those who would be employed in these buildings would be working in rooms or offices facing north. So the cruciform skyscrapers were then replaced by buildings in the form of a Y or of a spine.

I note here one further point. From the time of my first studies in town planning, "A Contemporary City of Three Million Inhabitants", shown at the *Salon d'Automne* in 1922, I had come to the conclusion that skyscrapers, whose height might well be fixed at the reasonable one of 220 metres, or about 700 ft., should be treated as office blocks and never as buildings for human habitation. Buildings for this latter purpose were limited to a height of 50 metres, or roughly 160 ft., and were never to be taller. Now, although these rules as to height have remained unchanged in any of my schemes over a period of twenty-five years, my adversaries regularly stir up public opinion by denouncing my dwellings of fifty storeys! Fifty metres and fifty storeys are two very different things, and public opinion would have reason to worry!

One more statement must be made: the book of 1924, now reprinted, includes the "Voisin Plan" for Paris, which provided for a number of skyscrapers. Twenty years after, the result of studies much more closely approaching the realities of the situation has been the reduction of the number of these office buildings to four, spaced at a distance of 400 metres from one another and placed outside all the historical sections of the city: they are built on the plain which stretches towards St. Denis between the hill at Montmartre and the *Buttes-Chaumont*. I think that my views in 1945 should outweigh the plan of 1924. At that time the main point was to establish a principle of town planning, and the whole book did in fact develop this true principle: that of the restoration of its rights and responsibilities to the centre of Paris.

The precise mixture of ingredients and the appropriate measures could not at that time be determined. The intervening years have quite naturally affected a clarification, and the detailed solution of the problem has become clearer, little by little, and the treatment of the site more established. In the turmoil of life and its accidents, the world tries to know itself: and much the same may be said in regard to town planning also . . .

Honest and sincere people, whether they represent technical or general public opinion, are not prepared to pass judgment on a doctrine before they understand its elements and its synthesis. As far as I am concerned, these elements first appeared in *l'Esprit Nouveau* from 1919 to 1925. Further points were successively dealt with in *Précisions* of 1930, in *La Ville Radieuse* of 1935, in *Des Canons, Des Munitions* . . . of 1938. in *Quand Les Cathédrales Etaient Blanches* of 1937, in *Sur les 4 Routes* of 1941, in *La Maison des Hommes* of 1942, in *La Charte d'Athènes* of 1943, in the studies for *l'Ascoral* which are beginning to appear in this year of 1945 (*Les Trois Establisements Humains* and *Manière de Penser l'Urbanisme*): and finally in the specialised works whose publication has been held up by events, *Plan de Buenos-Aires*, 1941, and *Plan Directeur d'Alger*, 1942.

This evolution has become more definite still this year, by the working out of several plans for towns or districts for which I am responsible, and in which the principles which were first enunciated in *Urbanisme*, in 1924, are now translated into action.

Principles, moreover, which have never been departed from.

Paris, November 1945.

LE CORBUSIER

INTRODUCTION TO 1971 EDITION

That a town is a tool (the opening statement of this book) is the basis of all modern town-planning; indeed of all local government, whose role it is to provide the power that a tool of this kind needs in order to operate. But the conception of a city as a vast productive machine, serving bodies and souls at the same time, is a fairly recent one. It is put forward positively and uncompromisingly in Le Corbusier's *The City of Tomorrow*, and the fact that we now look at towns and cities as working organisms, and feel an obligation to try to control them, we owe to a great extent to him and to this book.

Le Corbusier's great and deserved reputation as a prophet has made many people think of his ideas as belonging more to the realm of speculation than of practice. But he was concerned with the city as he found it, and was a realist as well as a visionary. The translated title of this epoch-making book suggests only conjecture about the future, but the original French title was simply *Urbanisme*, and it was on town-design as practised in 1924, when the book was written, that Le Corbusier's acute analysis is focused.

That is the context—the context of the utterly disorganized city structure, growing by accretion only and with no conception of planning control as a regular and recognized practice—within which we must assess Le Corbusier's insistence, in this book, on the geometrical basis of the well laid-out city. "A modern city", he said, "lives by the straight line . . . The curve is ruinous, difficult and dangerous; it is a paralysing thing." And elsewhere in the book: "We must have the courage to view the rectilinear cities of America with admiration."

In making such a declaration, however, Le Corbusier was not only opposing the *laissez faire* attitude to city growth of his own day, but was anticipating the present-day reaction—which has taken place since controlling cities became a vast bureaucratic business—in favour of informality and the exploitation of the historical accident. In 1924 the cult of the Picturesque and the writings of Jane Jacobs were all far in the future, but Le Corbusier felt that the real antithesis was not between order and the disorder produced by total anarchy, but between the geometrical kinds of order which have always determined architectural criteria and deliberate pursuit of the elusive goals of flexibility and informality. Running right through this book is a scornful denunciation of the cult of the informal in the person of Camillo Sitte, to whose writings and principles the book repeatedly refers. Le Corbusier regarded pursuit of the picturesque as an abdication of the responsibility to impose discipline for which the architect is trained.

We fancy nowadays that we have exposed the limitations of reliance on strict geometry such as this book puts forward, and in the sense that we have learnt to value variety and historical continuity, to believe that cities should preserve the capacity to change and above all that a city plan is not the end product of a designing process but the starting-point of a never-ending process in which many besides the designer must participate—in this sense Le Corbusier's diagnosis may seem simplistic.

But he was a brilliant polemicist as well as a brilliant architect, and knew well that an underlying discipline needed driving home firmly before any more flexible design policy became practicable. *The City of Tomorrow* was a pioneer work, and if it had not been for such unprecedented designs as those Le Corbusier puts forward in it (and a very few others like Tony Garnier's design of twenty years earlier for an industrial city), the progress made since would not have been possible. They provided the solid platform on which subsequent generations have been able to build—even though with a different emphasis from the one he recommended—because the intellectual discipline that planning needs was there clearly established.

The very precise delineation of built form with which Le Corbusier accompanied his statement of principles over-emphasized the limitations of his ideas by giving them an appearance of rigidity. These, too, must be looked at in relation to their time. As Le Corbusier's own buildings prove, he was himself a romantic as well as a rationalist, and there is no very great difference between his sensibilities and those which inspired the writings of Camillo Sitte, which he felt called upon to deride. The differences are partly those of tactics and of timing.

Le Corbusier's genius was to combine a passion for order with his extreme romantic sensibility, and however complex, multi-disciplinary and socially conscious the art of city-planning has now become, it must still refer back continually to his insistence on the need for an orderly framework. The more city-planning becomes a matter for other specialists than the architect, the more need is there for the architect's basic disciplines. The more latitude we rightly give the citizen to play a part in creating his own environment, the more need is there for one guiding hand to avert a free-for-all that can only result in chaos.

Le Corbusier's city-planning gospel is not, in any case, as simplistic as is often supposed. In this book there repeatedly occur, overshadowed perhaps by his challenging generalizations, statements, comments and criticisms that strike a completely contemporary note and indicate his awareness of the same environmental problems that we are occupied with today. He saw further ahead than we may think.

"At what rate", he asks, "do the trees that border our present streets wither and die as a result of the gases given off by petrol . . . ?"

"What sort of curve would the nervous system of an inhabitant of the great city show during, say, the last ten years ?"

"We must require the legal establishment of that absolute necessity, a . . . reserved zone of woods and fields."

"Town-planning . . . has become a sort of dumping ground for every difficult and unresolved problem such as the birth-rate, the social equilibrium, alcoholism, crime, the morals of the great city, civic affairs and so forth." This last sentence might have been written today.

And even on the ever-present subject of commuter-traffic Le Corbusier was aware of the growing problem. The motor-car had not yet become the menace it is now, and he refers to the railway termini as having replaced the openings in the medieval walls as the gateways to the city. But, he asks, "What, at the rush hours, are the numbers of travellers from the suburbs disgorged at each station?" (a question never asked by Camillo Sitte), and he is clearly aware of the direction in which things are going. He illustrates Hénard's prophetic project of 1906 for a traffic roundabout (*carrefour à giration: mouvement continu des voitures*)—perhaps the first of its kind—and comments on the huge build-up of motor traffic since then: "We must create vast and sheltered public parking places where cars can be left during working hours"—this in 1924.

He also says that high building cannot be isolated from questions of road and transport planning—and we would have been saved much discomfort if that principle had been regularly observed between 1924 and now—but he insists at the same time that the place to start rebuilding our present chaotic cities is the centre, and that "We must build on a clear site". In this, admittedly, he is out of step with our present, more humanly orientated, preference for conservation, for historical continuity, for rehabilitation rather than sweeping the old and obsolete away and starting afresh.

Nevertheless, his sympathy with what we now call conservation—the retention, as a totality, of areas of established character that still offer a valid environment—is clear from many of his books; for example from *When the Cathedrals were White* in which, writing of America, he says, "I like those vast and handsome hotels which are not at all modern in style but which have acquired a past through their richness and substantiality. There are living and dead pasts. Some pasts are the liveliest instigators of the present and the best springboards into the future."

Le Corbusier wrote with the courage of his convictions and, it must be repeated, was concerned, at the time when he wrote, with issuing a challenge. He was a convinced enough propagandist to stand up to any criticism. The first English translation of this book, appearing in 1927, incorporated his Voisin plan for Paris which had been exhibited at the Paris exhibition of 1925 and named after the Voisin motor-car company that had agreed to sponsor it after the Peugeot and Citroën companies had turned it down. The plan caused outrage, and Le Corbusier quotes and answers some of his critics. "Is the next generation really destined to pass its existence in these immense geometrical barracks . . . conveyed at the same hours by the same trains to the same skyscrapers, into identically similar offices?" wrote *L'Architecte*. But Le Corbusier gave as good as he got, and his scornful answer shows that, unlike many prophets, he was not without humour. "You are not going to make me believe", he wrote in the second edition, "that up to the fatal moment when my book was published trains started at any old hour, arrived when they liked, and once arrived were broken up and burnt, so that *other* trains could be employed the next day". Once involved with the machine age, he was deeply convinced, we must accept both the machine and what it can do for us. A period sentiment perhaps, but not a misconceived one. It needed stressing in 1924 and must remain an essential part of our philosophy in spite of the multiplicity of matters we are now aware that we must also stress.

J. M. Richards
30-11-1970

A TYPICAL LONDON SUBURB

A charming picture which displays every vice of planning!

FOREWORD

" In coveting the elemental
truths the soul destroys
itself, but if it goes to
earth, then it grows fat."
Max Jacob,
Phil., No. 1, 1924.

A TOWN *is a tool.*

Towns no longer fulfil this function. They are ineffectual; they use up our bodies, they thwart our souls.

The lack of order to be found everywhere in them offends us ; their degradation wounds our self-esteem and humiliates our sense of dignity.

They are not worthy of the age ; they are no longer worthy of us.

*

A city !

It is the grip of man upon nature. It is a human operation directed against nature, a human organism both for protection and for work. It is a creation.

Poetry also is a human act—the harmonious relationships between perceived images. All the poetry we find in nature is but the creation of our own spirit. A town is a mighty image which stirs our minds. Why should not the town be, even to-day, a source of poetry?

*

Geometry is the means, created by ourselves, whereby we perceive the external world and express the world within us.

Geometry is the foundation.

It is also the material basis on which we build those symbols which represent to us perfection and the divine.

It brings with it the noble joys of mathematics.

Machinery is the result of geometry. The age in which we live is therefore essentially a geometrical one; all its ideas are orientated in the

I

direction of geometry. Modern art and thought—after a century of analysis—are now seeking beyond what is merely accidental ; geometry leads them to mathematical forms, a more and more generalized attitude.

✳

The DWELLING *again puts before us the architectural problem in the demand for totally new methods of building, the problem of new plans adapted to modern life, the problem of an æsthetic in harmony with the new spirit.*

✳

The moment comes when a widespread enthusiasm is capable of revolutionising an epoch.

Such an enthusiasm inspires deeds and gives them a particular colour ; in fact, it determines them.

To-day, our enthusiasm is for exactitude. An exactitude carried to its furthest limits and raised to an ideal : the search for perfection.

You cannot be at one and the same time a " defeatist" and desire exactness ; on the contrary, an obstinate courage is needed and great force of character. This age is no longer one in which it is possible to take things easy or to relax. It is held powerfully buttressed in action. You cannot be a " defeatist" and achieve anything at all (and stupidity and disillusionment are equally fatal) ; faith is necessary and confidence in the innate decency of people.

You cannot be a " defeatist" and have modern town planning as an ideal; for you will have to admit the fact that many accepted notions must be scrapped. But a time has now come when modern town planning can be conceived of as a possibility, for a widespread enthusiasm has been made dynamic by the most brutal necessities of our daily life. It is directed by a lofty desire for truth. The awakening spirit of man is already rearranging our social forms.

It would seem that certain repeated phenomena clearly point to a solution of a problem whose roots are deeply buried in the facts of statistics. A moment comes when a widespread enthusiasm is capable of revolutionising an epoch.

*

This book was written during the emptiness of a Paris summer. The temporary interruption in the life of a great city resulted in my thinking in the end that I was perhaps being carried away by the grandeur of my subject, that I was being swept beyond the borders of reality.

Then there came the autumn season. In the early evening twilight on the Champs Élysées it was as though the world had suddenly gone mad. After the emptiness of the summer, the traffic was more furious than ever. Day by day the fury of traffic grew. To leave your house meant that once you had crossed your threshold you were a possible sacrifice to death in the shape of innumerable motors. I think back twenty years, when I was a student; the road belonged to us then; we sang in it and argued in it, while the horse-'bus swept calmly along.

On that 1st day of October, on the Champs Élysées, I was assisting at the titanic reawakening of a comparatively new phenomenon, which three months of summer had calmed down a little—traffic. Motors in all directions, going at all speeds. I was overwhelmed, an enthusiastic rapture filled me. Not the rapture of the shining coachwork under the gleaming lights, but the rapture of power. The simple and ingenuous pleasure of being in the centre of so much power, so much speed. We are a part of it. We are part of that race whose dawn is just awakening. We have confidence in this new society, which will in the end arrive at a magnificent expression of its power. We believe in it.

Its power is like a torrent swollen by storms; a destructive fury.

The city is crumbling, it cannot last much longer ; its time is past. It is too old. The torrent can no longer keep to its bed. It is a kind of cataclysm. It is something utterly abnormal, and the disequilibrium grows day by day.

We are, all of us, aware of the danger now. We may note in passing that in these few years we have all forgotten the joy of being alive, the everyday happiness of walking peacefully on one's legs; all our being is now absorbed in living like hunted animals a daily sauve qui peut ; [1] *everything is changed, the norm of our existence is completely demolished and reversed.*

Various timid remedies are suggested. . . . We all know the childish ardour with which, in haste and terror, the inhabitants of villages rush up improvised barrages to dam a torrent swollen by storm, which is already carrying destruction in its menacing swirl.

*

Fifteen years ago, in my wide travels, I felt the all-powerful might of architecture, but many and difficult stages were in front of me before I could find an adequate frame for it. Much of architecture lay buried deep under meaningless and incoherent traditions which had to be dug through before any enthusiasm could be evoked, and then only to a limited degree. On the other hand, when an architecture was genuinely appropriate to its environment it gave a pleasing sensation of harmony and was profoundly moving. Only when this was so, and without recourse to the text-books, did I feel the presence of one essential factor ; TOWN PLANNING, *a word I only learnt later.*

I devoted myself to this question.

Later, I read Camillo Sitte,[2] the Viennese writer, and was

---

[1] This is perfectly true; one risks one's life at every step. If you happened to slip, if sudden giddiness made you fall . . .

[2] Der " Staedtebau."

affected by his insidious pleas in the direction of the picturesque in town planning. Sitte's demonstrations were clever, his theories seemed adequate ; they were based on the past, and in fact WERE *the past, but a sentimental past on a small and pretty scale, like the little wayside flowers. His past was not that of the great periods, it was essentially one of compromise. Sitte's eloquence went well with that touching rehabilitation of " the home" which was later, paradoxically enough, to turn architecture away, in the most absurd fashion, from its proper path (" regionalism").*

When in 1922, at the request of the Salon d'Automne, *I made my panorama of a City of Three Million Inhabitants, I relied only on the sure paths of reason, and having absorbed the romanticism of the past, I felt able to give myself up to that of our own age, which I love.*

My friends, astonished to see me so deliberately passing over immediate considerations, said, " All this is for the year 2000 *!" Everywhere the journalists wrote of it as "The City of the Future." Yet I had called it " A Contemporary City"; contemporary because to-morrow belongs to nobody.*

I felt and knew that the solution was at hand. And see how rapidly things have moved during the years 1922 *to* 1925 *!*

In 1925, *the International Exhibition of Decorative Art in Paris demonstrated the uselessness of any turning back to the past. It marked the last and final pang before the world turns over a new leaf.*

Let us admit quite simply that after the futilities of the " sublime" there must come the serious work.

Decorative art is dead. Modern town planning comes to birth with a new architecture. By this immense step in evolution, so brutal and so overwhelming, we burn our bridges and break with the past.

*

Recently, a young and terribly disillusioned Viennese architect maintained that the death of old Europe was imminent; only young America could feed our hopes.

"There is no longer any problem of architecture in Europe," he said. "We have crawled along so far, overwhelmed and crushed by the overcharged burden of successive cultures. The Renaissance and the various Louis styles have worn us out. We are too rich, we are blasé, *we no longer have that virginity of mind which can raise up an architecture."*

The architectural problem of old Europe, I answered, lies in the great city of to-day. There lies the Yea or the Nay, life or slow extinction. One or the other, but it will be Yes if we wish it. *And our over-weighted cultures of the past will bring us, if we wish, the perfect solution proved by every trial and test of reason and delicate sensibility.*

*

Standing in front of my panorama of 1922, *the editor of the New York Magazine* "Broom" *said to me:*

"In two hundred years Americans will be coming over to Europe to admire the logical productions of modern France, while the French will be standing in astonishment before the romantic sky-scrapers of New York."

*

So we may conclude in this way:
Between belief and doubt it is better to believe.
Between action and dissolution it is better to act.
To be youthful and full of health is to have the power to produce much, *but years of experience are needed to produce* well.
The fact that we have been nourished by earlier civilizations enables us to disperse the clouds and to judge with clearness. It is "defeatist" to think that once one's student days are over one is nothing but a relic. Should we set out to be old? Old! The twentieth century in Europe may well be the magnificent ripening of a civilization. Old Europe is

not old at all. These are only words. Old Europe is still full of power. Our spirits, nourished by past ages, are alert and inventive ; their strength is in the head, while America's strength is in its arms and in the noble sentimentality of its youthfulness. If in America they feel and produce, here we think !

There is no reason why we should bury Old Europe.

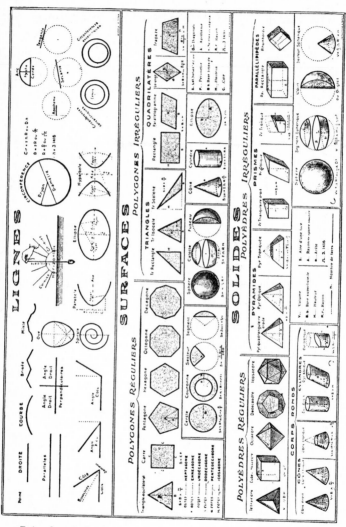

Printed on the backs of copy-books issued to the elementary schools of France. This is geometry.

FIRST PART
GENERAL CONSIDERATIONS

Man walks in a straight line because he has a goal and knows where he is going; he has made up his mind to reach some particular place and he goes straight to it.

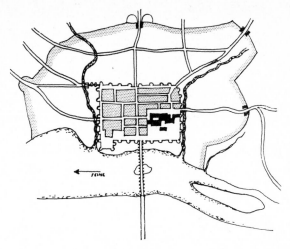

ROUEN IN THE TENTH CENTURY, BUILT ON THE
RECTILINEAR ROMAN PLAN

*The cathedral was built on the site of the ancient public buildings. In 1750
the new wall took in the neighbouring approaches ; the fate of the town was
decided. The heart of the city has remained rectilinear throughout the
ages.*

I

THE PACK-DONKEY'S WAY
AND MAN'S WAY

MAN walks in a straight line because he has a goal and knows
where he is going ; he has made up his mind to reach
some particular place and he goes straight to it.

The pack-donkey meanders along, meditates a little in his
scatter-brained and distracted fashion, he zigzags in order to
avoid the larger stones, or to ease the climb, or to gain a little
shade ; he takes the line of least resistance.

But man governs his feelings by his reason ; he keeps his
feelings and his instincts in check, subordinating them to the aim
he has in view. He rules the brute creation by his intelligence.
His intelligence formulates laws which are the product of

experience. His experience is born of work; man works in order that he may not perish. In order that production may be possible, a line of conduct is essential, the laws of experience must be obeyed. Man must consider the result in advance.

But the pack-donkey thinks of nothing at all, except what will save himself trouble.

*

The Pack-Donkey's Way is responsible for the plan of every continental city; including Paris, unfortunately.

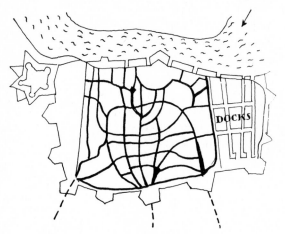

ANTWERP IN THE SEVENTEENTH CENTURY

The city has grown year by year, its plan being dictated by the existing roads leading to it. The result is an ingenious series of adaptations made during many centuries. None the less, the plan is a fine one of a curvilinear type.

In the areas into which little by little invading populations filtered, the covered wagon lumbered along at the mercy of bumps and hollows, of rocks or mire; a stream was an intimidating obstacle. In this way were born roads and tracks. At cross roads or along river banks the first huts were erected, the first houses and the first villages; the houses were planted along the tracks, along the Pack-Donkey's Way. The inhabitants built a fortified wall round and a town hall inside it. They legislated, they toiled, they lived, and always they respected the

Pack-Donkey's Way. Five centuries later another and larger enclosure was built, and five centuries later still a third yet greater. The places where the Pack-Donkey's Way entered the town became the City Gates and the Customs officers were installed there. The village has become a great capital; Paris, Rome, and Stamboul are based upon the Pack-Donkey's Way.

The great capitals have no arteries; they have only capillaries: further growth, therefore, implies sickness or death. In order to survive, their existence has for a long time been in the hands of surgeons who operate constantly.

The Romans were great legislators, great colonizers, great administrators. When they arrived at a place, at a cross roads or at a river bank, they took a square and set out the plan of a rectilinear town, so that it should be clear and well-arranged, easy to police and to clean, a place in which you could find your way about and stroll with comfort—the working town or the pleasure town (Pompeii). The square plan was in conformity with the dignity of the Roman citizen.

But at home, in Rome itself, with their eyes turned towards

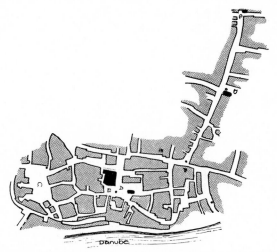

ULM : THE ANCIENT STRATIFIED ENCAMPMENT
Six centuries later, everything remains the same !

the Empire, they allowed themselves to be stifled by the
Pack-Donkey's Way. What an ironical situation ! The
wealthy, however, went far from the chaos of the town and
built their great and well-planned villas, such as Hadrian's
villa.

They were, with Louis XIV, the only great town-planners
of the West.

In the Middle Ages, overcome by the year 1000, men
accepted the leading of the pack-donkey, and long generations
endured it after. Louis XIV, after trying to tidy up the
Louvre (i.e. the Colonnade), became disgusted and took bold
measures : he built Versailles, where both town and château
were created in every detail in a rectilinear and well-planned
fashion ; the Observatoire, the Invalides and the Esplanade,
the Tuileries and the Champs Élysées, rose far from the chaos,
outside the town ;—all these were ordered and rectilinear.

The overcrowding had been exorcised. Everything else
followed, in a masterly way : the Champ de Mars, l'Étoile,
the avenues de Neuilly, de Vincennes, de Fontainebleau, etc.,
for succeeding generations to exploit.

But imperceptibly, as a result of carelessness, weakness
and anarchy, and by the system of " democratic " responsibilities, the old business of overcrowding began again.

And as if that were not enough, people began to desire
it ; they have even created it in invoking the laws of beauty !
The Pack-Donkey's Way has been made into a religion.

*

The movement arose in Germany as a result of a book by
Camille Sitte on town-planning, a most wilful piece of work ;
a glorification of the curved line and a specious demonstration
of its unrivalled beauties. Proof of this was advanced by the
example of all the beautiful towns of the Middle Ages ; the
author confounded the picturesque with the conditions vital
to the existence of a city. Quite recently whole quarters
have been constructed in Germany based on this *æsthetic*.
(For it was purely a question of æsthetics.)

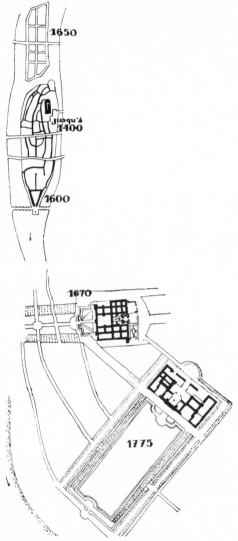

PARIS :   THE CITÉ, THE PLACE DAUPHINE, L'ÎLE SAINT-LOUIS,
THE INVALIDES, L'ÉCOLE MILITAIRE

*A significant diagram. These outline drawings, which are all to the same scale,
show the trend towards order. The town is being policed, culture is manifesting
itself and Man is able to create.*

This was an appalling and paradoxical misconception in an age of motor-cars. " So much the better," said a great authority to me, one of those who direct and elaborate the plans for the extension of Paris ; " motors will be completely held up ! "

But a modern city lives by the straight line, inevitably ; for the construction of buildings, sewers and tunnels, highways, pavements. The circulation of traffic demands the straight

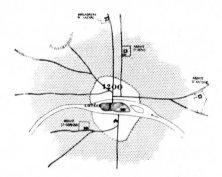

FIRST LUTETIA, THEN PARIS

The buildings still occupy the original sites, e.g. Notre-Dame, le Palais. *The great provincial roads, from north, east and south, from Issy, from Clichy, from the maritime provinces, and from the temple of Mercury (Montmartre), all remain.   Later, the Abbeys form definite landmarks.   As far as town planning is concerned, there is nothing but chance and the taking the line of least resistance.   Haussmann, later on, will open up and remodel the city to the best of his ability.   But it still remains based on the " Pack-Donkey's Way."*

line ; it is the proper thing for the heart of a city. The curve is ruinous, difficult and dangerous ; it is a paralyzing thing.

The straight line enters into all human history, into all human aim, into every human act.

We must have the courage to view the rectilinear cities of America with admiration. If the æsthete has not so far done so, the moralist, on the contrary, may well find more food for reflection than at first appears.

*

MINNEAPOLIS (A FRAGMENT)

This gives us an indication of a new moral outlook in social life, and provides some clue to the mutual astonishment which Americans and Europeans can cause one another to feel. Our epoch has now reached a stage in which the Old World must react to the new conditions and must consider the question of Town Planning.

WASHINGTON (A FRAGMENT)

A work of the mind. Here the victory is on the other side ; there were no more Pack-Donkey's Ways when this plan was designed, but instead there were Railways. The æsthetic problem still remains.

The winding road is the Pack-Donkey's Way, the straight road is man's way.

The winding road is the result of happy-go-lucky heedlessness, of looseness, lack of concentration and animality.

The straight road is a reaction, an action, a positive deed, the result of self-mastery. It is sane and noble.

A city is a centre of intense life and effort.

A heedless people, or society, or town, in which effort is relaxed and is not concentrated, quickly becomes dissipated, overcome and absorbed by a nation or a society that goes to work in a positive way and controls itself.

It is in this way that cities sink to nothing and that ruling classes are overthrown.

*

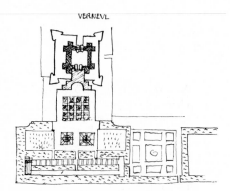

ANDROUET DU CERCEAU (RENAISSANCE)

The Artist and the Planner have been at work.

The right angle is the essential and sufficient implement of action, because it enables us to determine space with an absolute exactness.

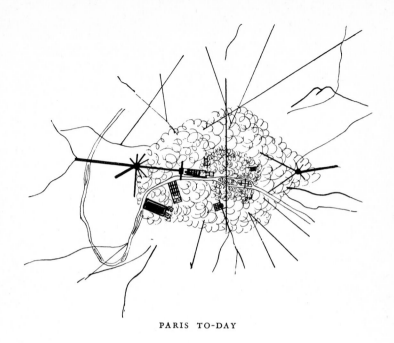

PARIS TO-DAY

II

ORDER

THE house, the street, the town, are points to which
human energy is directed : they should be ordered,
otherwise they counteract the fundamental principles round
which we revolve ; if they are not ordered, they oppose
themselves to us, they thwart us, as the nature all around us
thwarts us, though we have striven with it, and with it begin
each day a new struggle.

*

If I appear to be trying to force an already open door
(some people said this of my earlier book *Towards a New
Architecture*), it is because in this case also (I am speaking of
town planning) certain highly placed persons who occupy

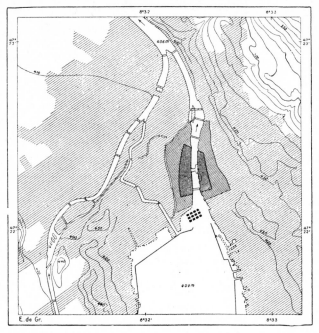

LAKE DWELLINGS (TURICUM)

strategic points on the battle-field of ideas and progress have shut these very doors, inspired by a spirit of reaction and a misplaced sentimentalism which is both dangerous and criminal. By means of every kind of quibble they try to hide from themselves and from others the lessons taught us by past ages, and to escape from the fatality and inevitability of human affairs and events. Our *march towards order* they would like us to believe to be only a child's attempt to walk or the folly of narrow minds.[1]

*

[1] From this angle I have been denounced in the *Temps* by M. Vaillat as a man who wishes to lead his fellow-architects into mad paths, as a *German* if you please !

" . . . But I would reply," he says, " to those architects, who may say that the time has come to submit to the logic of things, that the heart has its reasons which the mind cannot know. Satisfactions of an abstract nature are not, it may be, enough for our happiness; since we have in each of us an imperious need for

I repeat that man, by reason of his very nature, practises order ; that his actions and his thoughts are dictated by the straight line and the right angle, that the straight line is instinctive in him and that his mind apprehends it as a lofty objective.

Man, created by the universe, is the sum of that universe, as far as he himself is concerned ; he proceeds according to its laws and believes he can read them ; he has formulated them and made of them a coherent scheme, a rational body of knowledge on which he can act, adapt and produce. This knowledge does not put him in opposition to the universe ;

---

illogicality, for fantasy and grace.   The perfect town, the model village would bore us to tears. . . .

"My insistence on this point is not unimportant, for since the last *Salon d'Automne*, the theories of M. Le Corbusier in regard to the City of the Future have made great progress ; reviews, newspapers, and certain of my colleagues seem intoxicated by these seductive ideas which do not always, alas ! mean a seductive reality ; they do not seem to distinguish, poor fellows (and this is a characteristic of life itself), the plan of an old *French* house with its elegance, and its subtle arrangement, from the extreme monotony of the *German* plan." (*Le Temps*, 12 May, 1923.)

On principle, I generally avoid quoting an author for fear of giving a wrong impression.   But this quotation very clearly shows what seems to be M. Vaillat's doctrine and that of so many other people who are terrified by any simple statement of fact ; that doctrine is "Life" ; life with its many facets and unending variety ; life, two-faced or four-faced, putrescent or healthy, limpid or muddy ; the exact and the arbitary, logic and illogicality, the good God and the good Devil ; everything in confusion ; pour it all in, stir well and serve hot and label the pot "Life." That should be enough to make any living being a many-sided character of infinite variety.

Louis XIV and the Louvre, Le Notre and the Tuileries, the Invalides and Versailles and the Champs Élysées, all the gardens "à la française" ; we now learn that these are all German and the work of Germans !   But in the first place it seems to me wrong to talk of either Germans or Tonkinese when it is a question of creations of the mind.   And if M. Léandre Vaillat, who is on *Le Temps* (which is a serious paper) and in charge of the section devoted to town planning (which is a serious subject at this juncture), were better aware of the sources of his judgments he would realize that Latin history, and French history especially, are full of straight lines ; and that curves have always belonged rather to Germany and the countries of the North (baroque, rococo, disjointed Gothic, up to and including the plans of modern towns).   M. Léandre Vaillat and those with whom he shares his sympathies adore and put into practice in their town planning the curved line which has not been an ingredient in French architecture of the past, but which for twenty years has been a typical German manifestation.   Thus *Le Temps* (this serious newspaper) gives its readers false information by the medium of M. Léandre Vaillat, who is a charming man but apt to be over-excited by petty architectural sensations.

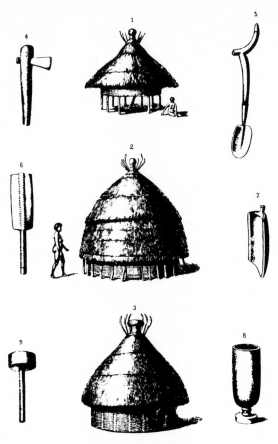

THE NATIVE HUT

it puts him in harmony with it ; he is therefore right to behave as he does, he could not act otherwise. What would happen if he were to invent a perfectly rational system in contradiction to the laws of nature, and tried to put his theoretic conceptions into practice in the world around him ? He would come to a full stop at the first step.

Nature presents itself to us as a chaos ; the vault of the heavens, the shapes of lakes and seas, the outlines of hills. The actual scene which lies before our eyes, with its kaleido-

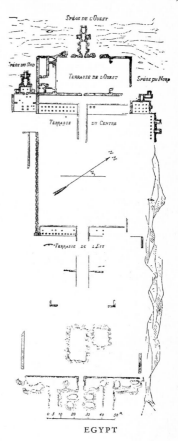

EGYPT

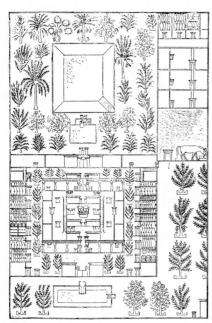

THE EGYPTIAN HOUSE

scopic fragments and its vague distances, is a confusion. There is nothing there that resembles the objects with which we surround ourselves, and which we have created. Seen by us without reference to any other thing, the aspects of Nature seem purely accidental.

But the spirit which animates Nature is a spirit of order; we come to *know* it. We differentiate between what we see and what we learn or know. Human toil is regulated by what we know. We therefore reject appearance and attach ourselves to the substance.

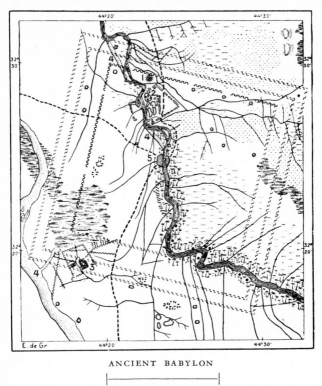

ANCIENT BABYLON

Dimension taken across Paris to the same scale.

For instance, I look at a man and he suggests to me a
fragmentary and arbitrary shape ; my idea of the man is not,
therefore, what I see at that moment, but what I know of him.
If he turns his face to me I do not see his back ; if he stretches
his hand out to me I do not see his fingers, nor his arm ; but
I know what his back is like and that he has five fingers and
two arms of a certain shape fitted for definite functions.

The laws of gravity seem to resolve for us the conflict of
forces and to maintain the universe in equilibrium ; as a
result of this we have the vertical. The horizon gives us the
horizontal, the line of the transcendental plane of immobility.
The vertical in conjunction with the horizontal gives us two

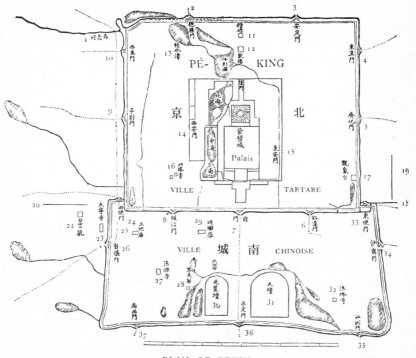

PLAN OF PEKIN

right angles. There is only one vertical, one horizontal; they are two constants. The right angle is as it were the sum of the forces which keep the world in equilibrium. There is only one right angle; but there is an infinitude of other angles. The right angle, therefore, has superior rights over other angles; it is unique and it is constant. In order to work, man has need of constants. Without them he could not put one foot before the other. The right angle is, it may be said, the essential and sufficient instrument of action because it enables us to determine space with an absolute exactness. The right angle is lawful, it is a part of our determinism, it is obligatory.

There, my friend the critic, is something to upset you.

I will go further, I will ask you this question : Look about you—look beyond the seas and across the centuries—and tell me if man has ever acted on anything but the right angle, and does there exist anything round you but right angles ? This is a very necessary inquiry ; pursue it and at least one fundamental point of the discussion will be settled.

Placed in the midst of a chaotic nature, man for his own security creates and surrounds himself with a zone of protection in harmony with what he is and what he thinks ; he needs a retreat, a citadel in which he can feel secure ; he

needs things whose existence he has himself determined. The things he makes for himself are a creation which contrasts all the more with his natural surroundings because its aim is closer to his mind, and further away and more detached from his body. We can say that the further human creations are removed from our immediate grasp, the more they tend to pure geometry ; a violin or a chair, things which come into close contact with the body, are of a less pure geometry ; but a town is pure geometry. When man is free, his tendency is towards pure geometry. It is then that he achieves what we call order.

Order is indispensable to him, otherwise his actions would be without coherence and could lead nowhere. And to it he brings the aid of his idea of perfection. The more this order is an exact one, the more happy he is, the more secure he feels. In his mind he sets up the framework of constructions based on the order which is imposed upon him by his body, and so he creates. All the works that man has achieved are an " ordering." Seen from the sky, they appear on the earth below as geometric objects. And if, on the most precipitous mountain, we construct a road climbing to a pass, that also has a clear geometric function and its windings are an exact and precise thing amid the surrounding chaos.

As we move higher in the scale of creation, so we move towards a more perfect order ; the result is the work of art. What an immense distance in degree and understanding between the hut of the savage and the Parthenon ! If the creation is ordered, it lasts throughout time and remains an object of admiration in every mind. This is the work of art, the human creation which, while no longer bearing any of the evident aspects of Nature, yet submits to the same laws.

Here is another thing, my friend the critic, which will horrify you very much indeed. Your amiable liking for twisted and mis-shapen objects is hurt by this crystal which

I am trying to make shine. You are not the only person who would like us to remain contented with essays in rustic bric-a-brac. In dealing with those who think as you do we must come back to town planning, for your and their negations would lead to the ruin of cities and districts and of entire countries; for you would like to deprive us of our proper environment and annihilate us. Man undermines and hacks at Nature. He opposes himself to her, he fights with her, he digs himself in. A childish but magnificent effort!

Man has always done this, and he has built his houses and his towns. Human order, a geometrical thing, reigns in

them, and has always done so; it is the mark of great civilizations, and has left dazzling landmarks to be our pride and for our perpetual admonition.

Your passion for twisted streets and twisted roofs shows your weakness and your limitation. You have no right to use the newspapers in order to impose your own stupidity and pretence on the more or less ignorant average reader.

*

The prehistoric lake village; the savage's hut; the Egyptian house and temple; Babylon, the legend of which is a synonym for magnificence; Pekin, that highly cultivated Chinese town; all these demonstrate, on the one hand, the right angle and the straight line which inevitably enter into every human act (for man, who has created his implements and has brought them to great perfection, sets out in practice from the right angle and finishes ideally with the right angle) : on the other hand, they are evidence of a spirit working right up to the limits of its own force and grandeur, and expressing itself in the right angle, which is obviously, geometrically, a perfect thing and at the same time its own proof of this ; a marvellously perfect figure, unique, constant and pure ; capable of being applied to ideas of glory and victory or to the idea of complete purity, the germ of every religion.

Paris is a dangerous magma of human beings gathered from every quarter by conquest, growth and immigration ; she is the eternal gipsy encampment from all the world's great roads ; Paris is the seat of a power and the home of a spirit which could enlighten the world ; she digs and hacks through her undergrowth, and out of these evils she is tending towards an ordered system of straight lines and right angles ; this reorganization is necessary to her vitality, health and permanence ; this clearing process is indispensable to the expression of her spirit, which is fundamentally limpid and beautiful.

*

If you were to look down from the sky on the confused and intricate surface of the earth, it would be seen that human effort is identical throughout the ages and at every point. Temples, towns and houses are cells of identical aspect, and are made to the human scale. One might say that the human animal is like the bee, a constructor of geometrical cells.

Of course we may admit at once that in the last hundred years a sudden, chaotic and sweeping invasion, unforeseen and overwhelming, has descended upon the great city ; we have been caught up in this, with all its baffling consequences, with the result that we have stood still and done nothing. The resultant chaos has brought it about that the Great City, which should be a phenomenon of power and energy, is to-day a menacing disaster, since it is no longer governed by the principles of geometry.

THE NOMADS' CAMP

THE NOMAD HAS TAKEN ROOT

*(and this is the sort of small town or village
which so delights the town planner !)*

WE ARE NO LONGER
NOMADS: WE MUST
BUILD TOWNS

In its sudden release, its superiority to mere will, its close har-
mony with the native gifts of a race, sensibility or feeling is a culmi-
nation and demands expression; it commands and leads men; it
determines their point of view and the deep meaning of things.

CUPOLA OF THE PANTHEON AT ROME (A.D. 100)

III

SENSIBILITY COMES INTO PLAY

THE Barbarians had descended, and had installed themselves among the ruin they had made, and in every Euro-
pean country these innumerable hordes began their barbaric
life and the slow rise of nations. Nothing remained of
antiquity but the mighty vestiges of Roman buildings.

From the covered wagon we must pass on to the temple
and the city. Roman cement has preserved the great domes,
the arches, the monolithic vaults, of which one side was
destroyed by fire but the other half still hangs suspended in
the void. Here is the exemplar; the rude craftsman of the
North is faced with classical culture.

For his buildings he takes a ready-made model. A savage
does not simply take over the alien fruits of another civilization. This will be made obvious. Man never copies, he is

unable to do so ; it would indeed be against all natural law. The fruits of civilization only ripen when all its technical resources are evolved, and these are the result of a slow accumulation of the mind's constructive efforts ; from zero man climbs to his highest point, passing sometimes painfully, sometimes easily, through the various intermediate stages : this is, in fact, the actual capital of a society, long in accumulating but sooner or later to be the nourishment of a spirit thus determined and claiming to shine forth and to be classed

ROMAN REMAINS, AFTER THE BARBARIAN INVASIONS

with the noblest epochs of this world. So we have this feeling of things which are rooted in profound acquired bases, which is what we mean when we use the word *culture*. There are certain moments when this feeling is so acute, its ingredients so resolved, it shines so crystal clear, that a mere word suffices to illuminate the whole question ; so we speak of Greek culture, Latin culture, Western culture and so on.

You cannot ransack another man's inheritance. No one has ever seen a cypress suddenly install itself, in full growth, in a forest of oak trees ; all that could be seen would be a tiny sapling taking two hundred years to grow into a fine tree. This is one of Nature's laws. You cannot absorb culture from text-books, or out of the treasures pillaged in great cities ; it implies centuries of effort.

So, to begin, the rude craftsmen of the North who wanted to copy the antique started out, like children, from what they saw, and not from what they knew. Their starting-point was the Pantheon, for this seemed good to them, but

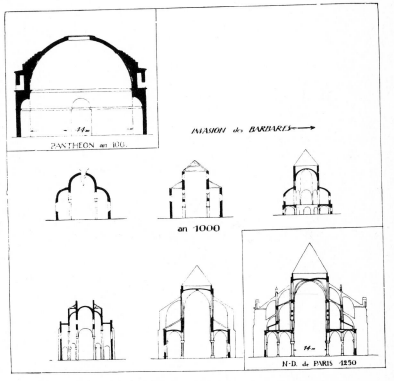

These sections, drawn to the same scale, show the point of departure and later results. In the Pantheon we have a summing-up of all the might of Roman equipment ; it stands for a plain and objective state of mind. Later there was a long technical struggle unwittingly dictated by a sensibility that was sometimes purely southern, sometimes northern. As the technical solution came nearer, the borrowed or traditional plastic elements were relinquished, and a whole category of new plastic elements, an exact expression of the aspirations of a people who had no longer anything in common with the Romans, was introduced.

their poor imitations fell to pieces; they knew nothing of the Roman cement, they had no technical means, no implements. They grew discouraged, and about the year 1000 they laid down their tools, resolved to do no more. If the priests

ROUEN CATHEDRAL

Here we have the Cathedral, with its pointed forms and jagged outlines, its evident desire for order; but lacking completely that calm and balance which witness to a maturer civilization.

no longer enjoyed their labour, at least they had their riches; they were expecting the end of the world—which did not arrive. Then was planted the seed of knowledge, and one age succeeded another. A technique was invented, tools were acquired, and as a result of this healthy discipline man's thought was brought to bear on the works of reason. A feeling was born, virgin and pure, true and real. In 1300 the cathedral was born !

Here is an amazing fact ! From the Pantheon [1] we arrive at the cathedral ; out of the old classical culture came the Middle Ages.

This is how cultures grow ; they are based on personal effort, on ingestion and digestion. When digestion has taken place, then we have acquired a feeling for things. And this very feeling is nourished by what has been ingested. There is no question of stealing when it is a question of the creations of the mind.

In its sudden release, its superiority to mere will, its close harmony with the native gifts of a race, sensibility or feeling is a culmination and demands expression ; it commands and leads men ; it determines their point of view and the deep meaning of things.

We leave the Pantheon ; but that is hardly true ! We arrive at the cathedral. From classical culture to the Middle Ages.

The Middle Ages. The Barbarian is there, with his striving after culture. This year of 1300 is not a culmination, the Barbarian is still too near at hand. The road continues. We too are on that same road and would wish to mark a further stage.

*

Sensibility comes into play. . . .

Sensibility or feeling is a categorical imperative which nothing can resist. Sensibility—some words have an odd fate—is precisely *not* a thing of the senses and it cannot be measured. It is something innate and violent ; a goad, an " urge." In weaker terms we might call it intuition.

But intuition, apart from simple manifestations of instinct, can be defined, for our comfort, on a basis of rational elements ; it might well be expressed by *intuition is the sum of acquired*

[1] I am here taking the Pantheon as a symbol of Roman construction generally.

knowledge. (And it might be said too of instinct that it is the sum of knowledge acquired through the ages.)

Here we have our feet firmly planted on the ground and in an environment where we can move freely and govern our own actions.

If intuition is the sum of acquired knowledge (which may go back a long way—atavism, the legacy of the ages, and so on), then feeling or sensibility is the emanation of these acquisitions. Its basis, therefore, is a rational one, and it is a rational fact; it is, that is to say, *what each man has earned for himself;* for every work has its reward.

You cannot steal another man's sensibility.

We must specify clearly if we are to bring together into one formidable array the various means which our own age has placed in our hands—that is to say, the equipment with which we must set up our framework for the work itself. We shall become conscious then of a feeling which is set free, and arising out of our small and fixed daily occupations, a sensibility which can lead them in the direction of an ideal form—towards a *style* (for style is a state of mind)—towards a culture, that is. These are the many-sided efforts of a society which feels it is ready for the crystallization of a new attitude after one of the most fruitful periods of preparation that mankind has ever known.

*

Culture manifests itself in a full realization of the equipment at our disposal, by choice, by classification, and by evolution. All this establishes a hierarchy of our sensibilities and so dictates the means by which these can be stimulated.

It is natural that, in seeking happiness, we should strive towards a sense of equilibrium. Equilibrium means calm, a mastery of the means at our disposal, clear vision, order, the satisfaction of the mind, scale and proportion—in fact it means creation. Disequilibrium witnesses to a state of conflict, to disquietude, to difficulties not resolved, to a state of bondage and of questioning. It is an inferior and earlier stage of preparation. Lack of balance is the equivalent of a state of fatigue, and balance the equivalent of a state of well-being.

So our classification might be as follows :

(a) The human animal, a primate with an animal's sagacity, its way of nosing things out and its instinct (which is for that matter an ancestral thing), creates for himself a state of equilibrium which is primitive and inferior no doubt, but which is perfect as far as it goes. Thus we can see the savage using pure geometrical forms, for instinctively he submits to those universal laws which he does not even try to understand, but from which he makes no attempt to liberate himself.

(b) Nations which are moving towards a culture (what force impels them ?) and emerging from their animal existence, arrive at a condition which involves a lack of equilibrium by reason of the successive leaps they take, in which, little by little, they acquire those convictions on which the brain can feed. The path is rough, here and there are rallying-points which can be recognized, but off the road there lie unknown gulfs, dangerous attempts and the inability to go further. And this effort, with its exuberances, its gaps, its excesses and its shortcomings, its lack of equilibrium, its absence of scale and proportion, wears them out.

(c) But the great moment is reached at length when every means has been proved, and where a complete equipment assures the perfect carrying out of rational schemes. A great calm is created by the power which has been acquired and which can be measured. The mind is able to create in a state of serenity. The period of struggle is over. The period of construction has arrived. And the spirit of construction has entered into our minds ; we are able to appreciate and to measure ; we can recognize what is best ; we can bring proportion to bear. From the welter of forms which were subjected to difficult trial we can make our choice of the purest forms. Our minds lead us to geometry. Our creations are not confused or hesitating, they are pure and formal. We can throw off our state of fatigue. We can create rational forms, with their basis in geometry; our trend is towards higher and more impartial gratifications, by reason of the mathematical spirit which inspires us; we can create in a detached and pure manner. Such are the epochs which we call classical.

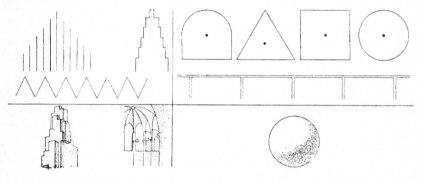

The various diagrams almost suffice in themselves to define the difference between Barbarism and Classicism. It is true that in either case man may attain to great things and move us by his works. All the same, one is of a more elevated order than the other, for one is complete where the other is only an attempt. One is a symbol of perfection, the other of effort only. One enchants us, the other startles us. Admitting that art is the great expression of human passion, yet none the less its mission is to lift us above disorder and by its power to give us an expression of equilibrium.

The physiology of the sensations : condition of peace.
       ,,   ,,   ,,   condition of fatigue.

Everything that proceeds from man, the creations of his hand or of his mind, express themselves by a system of forms which are, as it were, a transcription of the spirit which dictated their construction. Thus the various stages of civilization can be classified by forms; the straight line and the right angle cutting through the undergrowth of difficulty and ignorance are a clear manifestation of power and will.

Where the orthogonal is supreme, there we can read the height of a civilization. Cities can be seen emerging from the jumble of their streets, striving towards straight lines, and taking them as far as possible. When man begins to draw straight lines he bears witness that he has gained control of himself and that he has reached a condition of order. Culture is an orthogonal state of mind. Straight lines are not deliberately created. They are arrived at when man is strong enough,

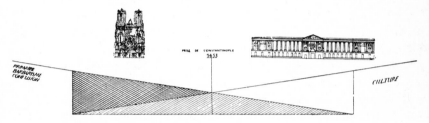

I do not speak disparagingly of the Cathedral. It merely occurred at its right date. The evolution of Western society did not cease at this moment as did the Roman after the Pantheon. Society was vowed to assiduous toil. The taking of Constantinople in 1453 poured over us the rays of Hellenism. The road leads on. Aspirations and painful ignorance give way to knowledge. A modified state of mind which was automatically translated into a system of ordered forms. Since Louis XIV two more centuries have passed. Through his equipment man is in a position to know everything that has happened in the world just as he has been able to acquaint himself with the whole of human effort in the past and the present. We are justified in believing that an even more delicate sensibility will come about, since our field of choice to-day is immense and we have the power to choose.

determined enough, sufficiently equipped and sufficiently enlightened to desire and to be able to trace straight lines. In the history of forms, the moment which sees the straight line is a climax; behind it and within it lie all the arduous effort which has made possible this manifestation of liberty.

*

A definition of modern feeling :
Our modern culture, acquired by the West, has its roots set deep in the invasions which extinguished antique culture.

After the check of A.D. 1000 it began to build itself again slowly through another ten centuries. With a primitive but admirably ingenious equipment invented in the Middle Ages, it inscribed certain points of great splendour in the eighteenth century. The nineteenth century was the most astonishing period of preparation known to history. Where the eighteenth century defined the fundamental principles of reason, the nineteenth century, by a magnificent effort, gave itself up to analysis and experiment and created an equipment which was entirely new, formidable, revolutionary and destined to revolutionize society. We are the heirs of that effort ; we are aware of our modern feeling and we know that an era of creation is about to commence. We are lucky in the possession of an equipment which is more efficient than ever before, and we are imperatively spurred on by this modern feeling.

This modern sentiment is a spirit of geometry, a spirit of construction and synthesis. Exactitude and order are its essential condition. Our means are such that exactitude and order are within our reach, and the unremitting toil which has given us the means of realization has created in us a sentiment which is an aspiration, an ideal, an unswerving tendency, an imperious need. This is the passion of our age. With what astonishment do we regard the spasmodic and disordered impulses of Romanticism ! A period in which the soul was thrown back on itself in such an effort of analysis that when it burst out it was as though a volcano were in eruption. No longer do we get these eruptions of an over-charged personality. The amplitude of our means impels us towards the general, and to an appreciation of the simple fact. In place of individualism and its fevered products, we prefer the commonplace, the everyday ; the rule to its exception. The everyday, the rule, the common rule seem to us now the strategic base for the journey towards progress and the beautiful. A general beauty draws us on and the heroically beautiful seems merely theatrical. We prefer Bach to Wagner, and the spirit that inspired the Pantheon to that which created the cathedral. We love the *solution*, and we are uneasy at the sight of failures, however grandiose or dramatic.

We behold with enthusiasm the noble plan of Babylon and we pay homage to the clear mind of Louis XIV ; we take his age as a landmark and consider the *Grand Roy* the first Western townplanner since the Romans.

Throughout the world we see the array of mighty powers, both in the industrial and in the social spheres ; we see, emerging from the chaos, ordered and logical aspirations, and we feel that they are in harmony with the means of realization we possess. New forms come to birth ; the world adopts a new attitude. The old prejudices crumble and crack and totter. Their imminent fall can be measured by the way in which they seek to hang on to this new impulse, by their anxiety to survive and to stifle a growth which is so dangerous to themselves. The force of the reaction reveals the force of the movement. An indescribable quiver is passing through everything ; it is putting the old machine out of gear ; it is the motive force and the aim of the age. A new age is beginning and new facts rise up.

So, to begin with, man needs a dwelling and a town. The dwelling and the town will result from the spirit of to-day, the modern spirit, this irresistible force, overflowing and uncontrollable now, but derived from the slow efforts of our forefathers.

It is a spirit born from the most arduous of all efforts, the most rational inquiry ; it is " a spirit of construction and synthesis guided by a clear conception."

*Left blank for a work
expressing modern feeling.*

Here is a fact which may seem discouraging at first blush, but one which on reflection will encourage and inspire confidence ; immense industrial undertakings do not need great men.

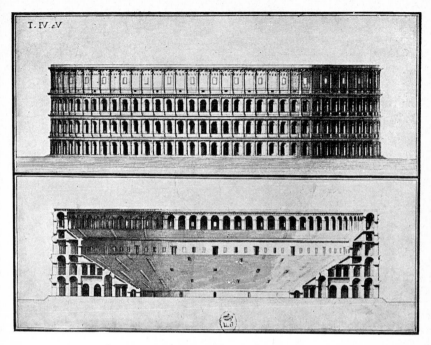

T. IV. & V

THE COLISEUM AT ROME

IV

PERMANENCE

HERE is a fact which may seem discouraging at first blush, but one which on reflection will encourage and inspire confidence: immense industrial undertakings do not require great men. Such works are carried out in the same way as rain fills a water-butt, drop by drop; and the men who bring them to completion are small, like raindrops, and not great like torrents. Nevertheless the achievement is a masterly one, and carries all before it like the torrent; the torrent exists apart from the individuals who exert themselves in it. The torrent is in *mankind*, it is not the individuals themselves. The industrial achievements of our own age which impress us so profoundly to-day are created by placid and modest men, whose thoughts are limited and direct, engineers who do their additions on ruled paper, who symbolize the forces of nature by α and β, and twist them into equations, placidly working their slide rules and reading there the banal figures which are so inevitable and fateful; yet these men can bring those of us who have something of the poet in us to the very extreme of enthusiasm and emotion. This is absolutely true and can be checked any day. It is most deceptive.

The point is that the products of reason must be most carefully differentiated from the products of passion. Actually,

THE STEAM ENGINE WHICH PEOPLE WENT TO SEE OF A SUNDAY
AT THE GARE DU NORD IN 1847

1923. *To the same scale, the engine of the express train which does the journey from Paris to Brussels in three hours.*

1847. *The " foaming steed "* . . .
1923. *The " magnificent steed "* . . .
1950. *The " superb steed "* . . .

The idea remains the same, right through the rise and decadence of a mechanical object.

however, there is always some sort of enthusiasm even in a
reasonable man, and that passion even the ultra-reasonable
man will put unawares into his slide rule, though it may be
a very tiny passion. Real passion is the thing that inspires
us to behave in ways that are not those of reason, passion
that is icy cold, or burning hot, meticulous or uncontrolled ;
it is the " potential " of the emotions which in the long run

1923.   NEW YORK

*The discovery of the New World.   It has been made a subject for the poet,
inspiring enthusiasm and admiration.   As for beauty, there is none at all.
There is only confusion, chaos and upheaval.   The unexpected reversal of all
our ideas excites us, but beauty is concerned with quite different things ; in
the first place, it has order for its basis.*

decides man's fate, and the determining emotions attached to
things. For we are so situated that through knowledge we
are bound always to go beyond the limits of our reason ;
reason is an open account stretching to infinity in which each
successive stage is registered ; not one tiny grain but adds
to it ; the individual perishes but the addition continues.
Human passion, since man was man, has been constant and

extends from birth to death; its range being limited by a maximum and a minimum reading which appear to us constant throughout the ages. This is the gauge by which we can measure the permanence of human creations.

The activity of the mind continues unendingly, in an ascending curve; it creates its implements; and this we call progress. The components of passion remain constant; they are low or high, coming between two limits which the ages have not altered. And we may risk the hypothesis that the greatest of emotive works, works of art, are born from a happy conjunction of passion and knowledge.

Men, in general, like the cogs of a wheel, appear to follow a path carefully marked for them. Their work is regular, fixed within narrow limits, their time-table is inexorable and exact; the year is divided into months as regards salary; into weeks as regards their Sunday rest, and into days as regards sleep; the hours are identical. Yet we have our Landrus and Soleillands, and at the same time how much moral splendour, as admirable as it is hidden. Man gets through his regular task and his additions; but still a flame, either small or fierce, burns somewhere in him; this is his emotional life. This it is that guides his destiny quite outside the product of his work, or the quality of that work. His work goes on adding itself up uninterruptedly, the tiny grain or the mighty rock, and the curve climbs up its steep track. But it is his passions that make war, that destroy or enrapture in the frantic chase for happiness: here is struggle, recoil, disaster or domination.

Generally speaking we are, in our passions, like wine in a barrel that is being transported from one place to another. We do not know at whose table we shall be served. The immense undertakings of humanity become more and more elaborated, more and more audacious and of a temerity that might well bring down the anger of the gods. Additions, the slide rule, squared paper, Bœotian calm. We shall have a clear example of it later, when we come to study " the means at our disposal." On the one hand, *an imbroglio of mediocre destinies;* on the other, the *hard and stern effort which goes forward under complete control towards magnificent results.* *It is all most deceptive.*

The poet stands there, judging and discerning the permanence of these enterprises ; he is at the opposite pole to addition sums, and the undulating curve he follows is that of the passions. Beyond utilitarian ends, he questions the imperishable : *man.*

The engineer is a pearl among men, we agree. But he is a pearl on a string, and the only other pearls he knows are his two *neighbours*, for his narrow researches lead him from an immediately anterior cause to a direct and immediate result. Your good engineer is a fixed being. The poet sees the whole necklace : he perceives individuals with their reasons and their passions ; behind them he sees the *thing we call man.*

AN HISTORICAL DOCUMENT ON A POST-CARD

Popular emotion !   A technical achievement evoking a poetical feeling.   But what sort of emotion and how long did it last ?

And man is capable of perfection ; theoretically there is nothing to prevent him reaching the sublime.

This divinity, this imperishable thing, has many times revealed itself, leaving a record by which we still may recognize the God we seek ; images of Negro gods, of Egyptian gods, Parthenons, great music. . . .

These are the things that really matter, that endure.

Up till now (*i.e.* in the nineteenth century) our equipment was so unreliable, so far from perfection, that it could not engross the attention to the exclusion of passion, which presented itself as a quite other phenomenon. But an immense revolution has taken place, the first in the annals of humanity, and it has completely upset our equilibrium ; it has trampled on our joys and has left in us only the bitterness of things for ever lost, and the disquietude of a future which still remains dark to us. Suddenly we find ourselves equipped with a fabulous battery of tools, so powerful, so brilliant that it completely upsets our standards of admiration and is likely to disturb age-long classifications. Too many magnificent events assail us in too short a space of time : our judgments waver, our values are topsy-turvy and we may end by becoming ridiculous. We are in a state of expectation : shall it be reason ? or shall it be passion ? here are two streams of thought, two individual things in conflict ; one looking back, the other forward ; the poet might blanch at the ruins, but the other might well be assassinated.

We can leave slaves to their past, but for those whose trend is towards the conditions of to-day, the whole thing is too dazzling. These conditions tear man from his toil ; they are a sort of apotheosis of mathematical figures. It is the age of steel, and the glitter of steel fascinates. The beauty of the machine is claimed as a new formula which will give results of a permanent order. But this is where error creeps in again. Let us analyze a few of the reasons why this is so, and after that I will give you proof of the sure and encouraging progress of human achievement ; so that after saying " how very disappointing," we can say " how very encouraging."

Let us attempt to formulate the standards of mechanical beauty. If we could admit that mechanical beauty was a matter of *pure reason*, the question would be settled out of hand : mechanical creation could have no permanent æsthetic value. Each piece of mechanism would be more beautiful

Here is the age of steel ; an age of confusion, of the introduction of a new scale confounding accepted standards, and causing great excitement, with good reason. Lyricism and the poetry of mathematics . . . but by 1920 the Great Wheel no longer existed ; the verdict had been passed and an idol overthrown.

than what had preceded it and would inevitably be surpassed by its successors. And so we should get an ephemeral beauty, soon out of date and despised. But in practice things do not happen so : man's sensibilities intervene in the midst of the most rigorous calculation. An engineer works out the section of a beam ; the inquiry into the strain it will bear gives him the coefficients of tension, resistance and inertia. But the coefficient of inertia is the product of the height and breadth of a beam chosen by himself. *Therefore he can choose a height* for his beam whose only justification may be his own pleasure; the breadth is a necessary consequence of that height. Here you have the intervention of an individual personal taste, sensibility and passion: the beam may be heavy or slender. If you extend the same considerations to more important undertakings you will realize the part played

A new spectacle. A new scale. New organs. The warning of a new epoch. The poet's foresight conceives the city on a new scale. With these proofs before him he knows that a great epoch is about to appear.

Homage to Eiffel! Fifty years have passed and people are still arguing for and against him; there are always perambulating corpses ready to attack some real thing: when our city is built on the same grand scale, then we shall be in a position to go into the question of the permanence of the Eiffel Tower.

by sensibility. Thus, of two machines giving the same results, you can say that one is more beautiful. By its lines you can distinguish whether a machine is French, German, American and so on. The machine begins to live, it has a form and a spirit, the likelihood of its being scrapped diminishes in proportion as the problem is lifted outside the realm of mere calculation. Its life will be as long as the ages grant it. The

locomotive that seemed to foam like a horse, the prancing
steed that evoked the hasty lyricism of Huysmans, is merely
rusty old iron on the scrap heap ; some motor-car of to-morrow
will involve the overthrow of some existing popular model.
But the Roman aqueduct remains, the Coliseum is still
piously conserved, the Pont du Gard remains. But will the
emotion produced in us by Eiffel's bridge at Garabit endure ?

THE PONT DU GARD.   ROMAN

Among the very great works of architecture, and going far beyond mere mathematical
formulæ.

Here mere reasoning no longer suffices, here we must suspend
judgment, which can only be formed by posterity ; at this
point we can only feel our ignorance of the future fate of
our great industrial enterprises.   Our enthusiasms are immense ;
in many cases they are rooted in vital and healthy instincts.
Where a man's passion for creation has taken form, his work
will endure through the ages.
    But this is a dangerous judgment, for shall we see engineers
trying to turn themselves into men of æsthetic sensibility ?

That would be the real danger : for their equipment would not develop further. An engineer should stay fixed, and remain a calculator, for his particular justification is to work within the confines of mere reason.

In these cases the only right of individual sensibility is to embody the collective will. Collective will is the state of mind of an epoch which is capable of application to the mass of men as well as to the individual, by means of those great

THE PONT DE GARABIT (DESIGNED BY EIFFEL)

successive movements which are at once an education, a disintegration, and a renewal ; it is something which cannot be adulterated, a mathematical medium which must be deeply important to us, since it provides for the multitude a single outlook and a unanimous sensibility. With a cold and clear accountancy the + and − of an epoch are established. A way of thinking, of general application, arises. And creations based on mere calculation, though they actually add nothing, yet find themselves borne along by the general stream of sensibility which has recovered the true human scale, through which man can measure his highest and his lowest.

So that before the products of calculation we stand face to face with a phenomenon of the highest poetic order ; it is not the individual who is responsible for it ; the adding of unit to unit has made up the necessary total. It is man who then realizes his potential powers. A platform raised by the mass of men over and above their individual circumscribed labours ; this is the style of an epoch.

All this is extremely encouraging. Man may create noble things.

Then there appear men of genius, who can start from the level of such a platform, to create imperishable works, images of Gods, or Parthenons.

The city is profoundly rooted in the realms of calculations. Engineers, nearly all of them, work for the city. And through them the necessary equipment for the city will come into being. This is the essential thing for that part of it which is utilitarian and consequently ephemeral.

But it is the city's business to make itself permanent ; and this depends on considerations other than those of calculations.

And it is only Architecture which can give all the things which go *beyond* calculation.

THE VILLA ROTONDA BY PALLADIO, AT VICENZA

Our constant aim, which we must pursue with patience and cunning, must be to throw out of action all the forces that make for the opposite of Joy—that is to say, Despair. Despairing Cities! The despair of cities!

PISA : CYLINDERS, SPHERES, CONES, CUBES

V

CLASSIFICATION AND CHOICE

(A SURVEY)

> " It is the city's business to make itself
> permanent, and this depends on considera-
> tions other than those of calculation. It
> is only Architecture which can give all the
> things which go beyond calculation."

LET us take the objective fact of the city and trace for a
moment the circle of the visual impressions and the optical
sensations which it gives rise to ; and let us see what effect
it has in regard to fatigue and well-being, cheerfulness or
depression, its capacity to ennoble and fill us with pride or
with indifference, disgust and revolt.

A city is a whirlpool ; let us classify the impressions it
gives rise to, inquire into our sensations arising therefrom and
choose among the methods which may relieve or effect a cure.

Let us deal first with the eye ; afterwards we can consider the ear, the lungs and our legs.

The eye perceives, the brain registers, the heart beats ; synchronous phenomena common to civilized man and beast alike.

After our examination of the things which affect us physically and agitate our hearts, we shall come to an important decision ; we shall come to consider as *more important* than the *mechanism* of the city, what we may call the *soul of the city*. The soul of the city is that part of it which is of no value from the practical side of existence : it is, quite simply, its poetry, a feeling which in itself is absolute, though it is so definitely a part of ourselves. The mechanism of a city is merely a matter of adaptation ; there is an approximation to perfection at happy moments, and we adjust ourselves as best we can to its difficulties, which in time vanish, as vanish, for that matter, the perfected mechanisms which to-morrow may be scrapped. Though I shall, later in this book, allocate

BYZANTIUM :   THE SEVEN TOWERS ;   HORIZONTALS WITH CENTRAL
AXIS.   WHITE MARBLE

a very important place to the mechanism of the city, it is most necessary to state now that this mechanical adjustment lies apart from the definite and profound feelings which belong to our emotions and sensibilities, which hold the secret of our happiness or our misery.

A form of town planning which preoccupied itself with our happiness or our misery and which attempted to create happiness and expel misery would be a noble service in this age of confusion. Such a preoccupation, creating its appropriate science, would imply an important evolution in the social system. It would denounce on the one hand the harsh and futile individualistic rush for egotistical gratification, by which our great cities have been created. It would show, on the other hand, that at the critical moment an automatic recovery had taken place ; that feelings of solidarity, pity and the desire for good had inspired a powerful will towards a clear, constructive and creative end. Man at certain periods takes up again the business of creation, and it is at such moments that he is happy.

STAMBOUL : THE SUAVE MELODY OF VERY GENTLE FORMS

PAIN OR PLEASURE

If we compare New York with Stamboul, we may say that
the one is a cataclysm and the other a terrestrial paradise.

New York is exciting and upsetting. So are the Alps ;
so is a tempest ; so is a battle. New York is not beautiful,
and if it stimulates our practical activities, it also wounds our
sense of happiness.

Let us make matters clear : two sensations affect us ; a
feeling of comfort and a feeling of discomfort. The last
chapter but one (*Sensibility Comes into Play*) gave us two
programmes : a state of barbarism and a state of classicism ;
the spiritual effects of a state of things to which we react
physiologically and which might be expressed thus : (*a*) a condition of comfort, and (*b*) a condition of discomfort. When-
ever the line is broken, jolted, irregular and constructed
without rhythm, or the form is over-acute or bristling, our
senses are painfully and grievously affected. Our spirits suffer
as a result of this confusion and harshness, this lack of " good
manners," and the word " barbarous " comes at once to the
mind. But when the line is continuous and regular, and the
forms are full and rounded without a break, and governed
by a clear guiding rule, then the senses are solaced, the mind
is ravished, liberated, lifted out of chaos and flooded with
light. Then the word " mastery " comes to the mind, it glows
brightly and we are happy.

Here is our true basis ; a physiological and irrefutable
one.

A city can overwhelm us with its broken lines ; the sky
is torn by its ragged outline. Where shall we find repose ?

In old cities famous for their beauty we walk among shapes
which are co-ordinated, designed around a centre or along an
axis.

Horizontals, magnificent prisms, pyramids, spheres and
cylinders. The eye sees them as pure forms and the mind

PERA

The serrated outline of the city of merchants, pirates and gold seekers.

STAMBOUL

The fervour of minarets, the calm of flattened domes. Allah watching over all, but orientally immutable.

ROME

Geometry, implacable order, war, organisation, civilisation.

SIENA

The anguished tumult of the Middle Ages. Hell and Heaven.

takes them in with delight and follows the precision of their lines. Here we have serenity and joy.

As you go North, the crocketed spires of the cathedrals reflect the agony of the flesh, the poignant dramas of the spirit, hell and purgatory ; and forests of pines seen through pale light and cold mist.

Our bodies demand sunshine.

There are certain shapes which cast shadows.

*

THE SYMPHONY

In the same way as the palate enjoys the variety of a well-arranged meal, so our eyes are ready for ordered delights. The relation between quantity and quality is such that, in functioning, they form integral parts of each other.

The eye should not always be stimulated in the same manner, or it becomes tired ; but give it the necessary " rotation " and change of scene and your walks will be neither tiring nor drowsy.

Behind the eye is that agile and generous, fecund, imaginative, logical and noble thing : the mind.

What you set before your eyes will create joy.

Multiply that joy ; it is the full attainment to which a man reaches by the use of all his talents. What a harvest !

Here is a wonderful mechanism that each of us can set in motion : knowledge and creation. We can create symphonies. To be soothed by certain forms, to realize how they were conceived, by what relationships they were brought together, how they answer to a need which has become articulate, how they rank in one's personal scheme of chosen images. To measure, to compare indeed ; to share with their creator his raptures and his torments. . . . Why do we make pilgrimages to beautiful cities if not to put gaiety into our mind and senses, if not to recognize by means of this witness in stone that

STAMBOUL : MUEZZINS, NARGHILES, TRANQUIL CEMETERIES

The past, the present, the beyond, the immutable. An elegy of prisms.

man is capable of grandeur ; and to feel in oneself the joy that such a certainty gives us ? For all our "trivialities," our comfort, money and the crease in our trousers, pale away before the rapture of such an assurance of noble feeling !

We must be careful lest we set in motion the opposite of joy—despair. Despairing Cities ! The despair of cities ! Oh ! municipal councillors, who have sown despair in your cities !

Alas ! how much of it there is.

*

BYZANTIUM : THE AQUEDUCT OF VALENS

An immense horizontal running through the surrounding country and forming a rigid backbone along the Seven Hills.

STAMBOUL

*Vertical forms, but based on pure prisms. A Hellenism unknown to the
Gothic.*

The city, through what it offers to the eyes, dispenses either
joy or despair ; a sense of something noble, pride or revolt,
disgust, indifference, happiness or fatigue.

And everything depends on a choice of forms. But we
are not concerned with a question of decked-out forms in
Louis XIV, Baroque or Gothic fashion, borrowed from the
ancient junk of dead and gone styles.

The city which is to be will contain *in itself* a formidable
mechanism, a powerful force, a workshop containing innumerable and precise implements, a harnessed tempest.

The forms we are discussing are the eternal forms of pure geometry and these will enshrine in a rhythm which will in the end be our own, going far beyond the confines of formulæ and charged with poetry, the implacable mechanism which will pulsate within it.

The eye is capable both of being battered into submission or of being stimulated.

The mind too may be sunk deep or lifted high.

I give *a problem of form* which should be entered in the agenda of all Municipal Councils : " A decision must be arrived at in regard to the prohibition of certain injurious forms and the encouragement of stimulating forms."

THE ISLAND OF TIBERIUS, AFTER AN OLD ENGRAVING

A Turkish proverb : Where one builds one plants trees.
. . . .
We *root them up.*

THE PROCURACIES, VENICE

The uniformity of the innumerable windows in this vast wall on the Piazza San Marco gives the same play as would the smooth side of a room. The repetition of the same unit lends the wall a grandeur that is boundless but can be easily appreciated ; the result is a type-form of a clear and simple nature. The pigeons of St. Mark's themselves add their own uniform module, providing a varied and effective note in the scheme.

VI

CLASSIFICATION AND CHOICE
(TIMELY DECISIONS)

" It is the city's business to make itself permanent, and this depends on considerations other than those of calculation. It is only Architecture which can give all the things which go beyond calculation."

SINCE we are now in a position to know how we feel, let us choose, for our comfort, the possible methods to effect a cure for the general well-being.

*

The city is a whirlpool, yet it is none the less a body with definitely placed organs, and it has a shape. The character, nature and structure of this body can be understood. The analysis of a city belongs to the realm of scientific investigation, its composition being coherent enough to determine its guiding principles.

By its geographical and topographical situation, from the political, economic, and social part played by it, the line of its evolution can be followed ; from its past, its present and the ferment at work within it, the curve of its development can be estimated. Statistics, graphs, are the a, b, c, and so on of an equation whose x and y can be calculated in advance with a certain approximation. At least the *general sense* of the answer given would be right, even if in actual application there were every likelihood of the solution being modified by unexpected developments. This *general sense* is of importance, for it endows us with some degree of foresight.

And the real essential is that we should be able to foresee ; and this is indispensable and urgent.

For in that case, in making decisions which may be useful for the moment, we can preserve a certain latitude in regard to future developments.

*

In the larger sense, the development of the city, since the direction lies in the hands of a single body such as a City Council, can give us a sense of unity and coherence ; and this is a reassuring thought.

But the details of this development involve the growth of individual cells (houses), each of which is an individual thing ; this tends to a lack of coherence, and is a grave menace. Perhaps this difficulty can never be altogether avoided, and its defects can only be combated by those weapons which belong to the function of Architecture in town planning. For example, by the grouping of cells in great families of the same species, such as exist in the *Rue de Rivoli*, the *Place Vendôme* and the *Place des Vosges* in Paris ; the *Procuracy* in Venice, and the *Carrière* and *Stanislas* in Nancy ; groupings of a rare quality, which definitely help to create a deep satisfaction in their inhabitants, and a lofty sentiment of civic virtue, not to mention the profit brought to the Travel Bureaux.

Thus the situation presents itself in this way : a degree of foresight as to general development, but a mass of unknown factors in the detailed development, these latter being a definite menace.

But the details are the whole city ; a detail in a city means a house multiplied a hundred thousand times ; therefore it is the city.

The condition of the whole city lies in the condition of each of its cells, and here we cannot foresee.

Whereas, in walking through a city our minds can estimate the value or the uselessness of the suggested general development in the future, and can appreciate a co-ordinated and noble plan, our eyes, on the contrary, are subject to the limitations of their visual field, and can only see cell after cell ; and the sight of these provides a jagged, loose, diversified, multiplied and nerve-wracking spectacle ; the sky is seen against a ragged outline and each house suggests, even by its very shape, some different order of thing. The eye is overwhelmed, tired and hurt; and the plans which seemed so magnificent are apprehended, after such a preliminary experience, by a mind bewildered and worn out and indisposed for its task.

This is the critical point to which our analysis of the city brings us ; the spectacle of individualism run riot, fatal and inevitable. A weariness arising out of chaos ! There is, and there will be, no common standard until such time as a new age of discipline, wisdom and unanimity in the sphere of art, is born.

We must beware of a rash optimism, rather let us admit the worst ; and this is nowadays our daily fare.

So we reach the following conclusions :

If a common standard determined these cosmopolitan cells, disorder would be exorcised, the scene presented to us would be one of order, and peace would return.

If we could but achieve unity in detail, the mind would be free to consider, with a new and lively interest, a noble lay-out of the whole city.

We have now formulated an ideal and precise aim. Already, in the time of Louis XIV, the Abbé Laugier had propounded the following axioms :

1. *Chaos, disorder and a wild variety in the general lay-out* (*i.e.* a composition rich in contrapuntal elements like a fugue or symphony).

2. *Uniformity in detail* (*i.e.* reticence, decency, " alignment " in detail).

*

Present-day reality does not accord with the first of these axioms ; since those who make our bye-laws for us demand streets which can never be anything but corridors.

And it gives us the contrary of our second axiom ; for we are constantly assailed by incongruous details.

And our decorative town planners, the lovers of beautiful detail and of highly individual shop-fronts and so on, thrust us still deeper into error. (They are really, in a sense, before their time, which will come later, though their programme needs modification.)

Past realities do fit in with our axioms, as far as the so-called " art " cities are concerned : Bruges, Venice, Pompeii, Rome, old Paris, Siena, Stamboul and the rest : here we find a certain largeness of conception in the general lay-out, and a remarkable uniformity of detail. *Yes, of detail!* In those fortunate epochs the methods of construction were uniform. Right up to the nineteenth century, a window, a door were " holes for men," that is to say, elements on the human scale : roofs were constructed according to universally admitted and excellent precedents. The style of building was that of a most praiseworthy perfection, of a good technical finish, and an economy in the methods of building; the result of this was that every house was of the same tribe, family and blood. They had an astonishing unity. In Stamboul every dwelling is of wood, every roof is of the same pitch, and covered with the same kind of tile. All the great buildings, mosques, temples, caravanserais, are of stone. The basis of all this is

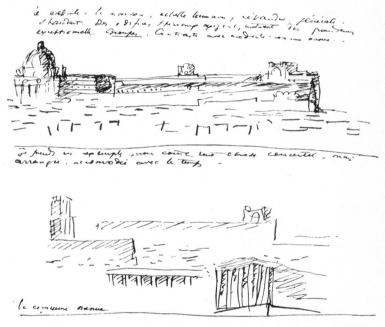

Against a background of houses, that is to say, of elements of the same kind, Rome raises high its palaces and its temples. They stand out from the rest. Architecture disengaging itself from the urban confusion.

the existence of a standard. So at Rome and at Venice; all the dwelling-houses are stuccoed; at Siena they are of brick; the windows are to one scale, the roofs of the same pitch and covered with the same tiles; the colour is uniform. Palaces and churches are of gold and marble, sculptured and ennobled (though not always) by " divine proportion." The whole matter is clear. In Turkey, Italy, France, Bavaria, Hungary,

Serbia, Switzerland, Russia, everywhere before the disturbing influences of the nineteenth century, men's houses were boxes of the same nature, and even the passage of time has modified them but little according as advancing culture and the means at their disposal required and permitted of modification in quality. *There was a universal standard and complete uniformity in detail.*

Under such conditions the mind is calm.

Ideas of planning on a noble scale can then make themselves heard.

*

UNIFORMITY IN DETAIL

Everything to-day urges us, and indeed impels us, in this direction. The present social evolution itself is bridging the distance between the great house and the cottage.

To-day the rich man is moving towards simplicity, since exterior show counts for so much less ; and the poor man grows more and more established in his rights. Some sort of stability is being established and centres round a cell based on the human scale ; and the industrial enterprise of to-morrow which has almost arrived [1] can only be achieved by the use of uniform elements. And these elements tend towards a general uniformity.[2]

[1] *I.e.* the industrialization of the builder's yard.

[2] An important event has taken place : the universal use of reinforced concrete. This new weapon offers the inventor and designer new solutions of the utmost importance; thus the attic can be done away with and replaced by a terrace. The roof, therefore, becomes habitable, and more than that, becomes a sort of extra street, a place for strolling. The profile of the street, determined by the outlines of the houses against the sky, would then dispense with dormers, eaves, mansards and the rest, all of which are elements which contribute to disorder from the plastic point of view. These would be replaced by a pure and simple line. Now the silhouette of houses seen against the sky is one of the most fundamental elements in urban æsthetics ; *it is a thing that strikes the eye at the first glance and gives the final impression.* Thus a street which had one uniform cornice seen against the sky would be a most important advance towards a noble architecture. If only we could insert such an innovation on the agendas of town councils, we should be adding enormously to the happiness of the inhabitants. We must always remember that the fates of cities are decided in the Town Hall; municipal councils decide the destinies of town planning.

Based on this uniform web, we shall have an eloquent and noble general lay-out.

To put it shortly : if the builder's yard is to be industrialized, it must pass from an anachronistic construction of single dwellings " to the requirements of clients," to the construction of whole streets, indeed of whole districts. We must, therefore, analyze closely the " cell," that is to say, the house ; we must fix its scale, and proceed to its construction in a

PARIS : THE PLACE DES VOSGES

uniform series, *i.e.* by mass-production. The repetitive and tranquil framework created thus from innumerable cells would lead up to great architectural schemes, far removed from our wretched corridors of streets ; town planning would abandon the " corridor-street " of to-day, and by laying down new plans it would create on a vast scale of another kind the architectural symphony it must be our aim to bring about.

The " corridor-street " between its two pavements, stifled between tall houses, must disappear. Cities can be something better than palaces which are all corridors.

Town planning demands uniformity in detail and a sense of movement in the general lay-out.

These ideas are almost enough to get us all turned out!

*

We shall not find disciples all at once. It will be a long time before a standard and a common measure will bother very much those architects whose whole careers consist in

In Venice the common measure of the ordinary quarters of the town causes the more splendid squares and places to " stand out " in a lively fashion.

recalling in their work the archæological lessons they learnt in their youth.

But there is another point.

A bold glance into the future suggests that the " tentacular " cities will be reorganized out of their decrepit structure by enormous schemes of planning ; elements on a scale hitherto undreamed of will achieve sublime masses : New York, which is a barbarian city, has provided the inevitable means, the *sky-scraper;* steel, reinforced concrete . . . and all that goes with these ; all that goes to make up the building, light, air, heat and hygiene ; and beyond that a large-scale indus-trialism slowly elaborating its means, and inventing new ones, on a scale hitherto unknown. The twentieth century still wears the clothes of pre-mechanical humanity. It is as though public economy, commerce, politics and finance were still governed by the post-boy with his horses and his relays. The awakening of the twentieth century will be an amazing thing ; at least it would seem so to us, if to-morrow we were to find the new city an accomplished fact. But the conception will progress by easy stages, and one day unawares we shall find ourselves transplanted into the new city.

To the left of the Golden Horn is Pera, on the right Stamboul. Pera is Genoese, and bristling with tall, cramped, vertical houses ; the checkered pattern of the windows gives a weighty cohesion to the mass. But the spread-ing red roofs of Stamboul are like a sea from which the mosques rise up serenely in their sculptural whiteness.

The cells (dwellings) will be poised in buildings twenty, forty and sixty storeys high.[1] But man, whose average height is 5 ft. 8 in., an arrangement that cannot be altered, will have some difficulty in adapting himself to the vast constructions of his city. Therefore we must furnish the painful void of this too great disparity by introducing, between mankind and his city, some proportional mean which will relate both measures and reduce them to a common scale. Suppose we could find hidden somewhere in the files of the town planner some *proportional mean* which would completely satisfy

[1] I have recently received a photograph of a scheme for a monster hotel in the United States which has 180 storeys !

man's accustomed needs, and bring him joy, recreation, beauty and health !

We must plant trees!

But whether we achieve the happy realization of a common architectural measure, a pure " module " of architectural invention adapted to the new period, or whether we continue in our physical discomfort and a wretched and selfish individualism, the tree in any case helps our physical and spiritual well-being.

STAMBOUL

Trees everywhere, and rising from among them noble examples of architecture.

Why should not the new spirit in architecture, that fast-approaching town planning on the grand scale which we have talked about so much, satisfy the deepest human desires by once more covering with verdure the urban landscape and setting Nature in the midst of our labour ? [1] so that our hearts might find some reassurance in face of the dreadful menace of the great city which imprisons, stifles and asphyxiates

[1] A Turkish proverb says : Where one builds, one plants trees. With us they are uprooted. Stamboul is an orchard ; our towns are stone quarries.

those who are cast into it and who have to work in it ; for work is a noble necessity which should bring peace to the mind and lead on to the rapture of creation.

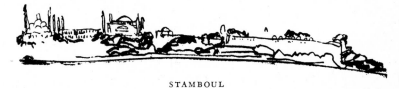

STAMBOUL

Everywhere the houses are surrounded by trees ; a charming partnership between man and nature.

The gigantic phenomenon of the great city of to-morrow will be developed amid pleasant verdure. Unity in detail ; a

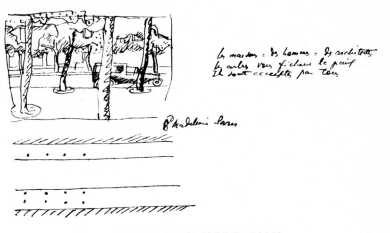

BOULEVARD DE LA MADELEINE, PARIS

The boulevard of to-day : here there is on one side a double row of trees. Viel, who runs his restaurant here, is well aware of the value of his oasis in contemporary Paris. A slight indication of a matter of very great importance.

magnificent " tumult " in the whole ; a common human measure and a proportional " mean " between the fact " man " and the fact " nature." This is what we need.

The architecture which is to be will have its beauties, born of a noble enthusiasm, and these will be so placed by the town planner of the future that a studied calm, surprise, amazement or joy of discovery will lend them the value they were intended to possess.

This is not Chantilly nor Rambouillet, but the Parc Monceau *at Paris. Here is a clear aim before us : the City of To-morrow could be set entirely in the midst of green open spaces. The mistake made in New York was that the sky-scrapers were not built in the parks. I shall be told that this is Utopian, but I am quite ready to take up the challenge.*

" *And what about motor-cars?* "

" *So much the better,*" replied the Great *Authority :* " *they will no longer be able to run in the streets.*"

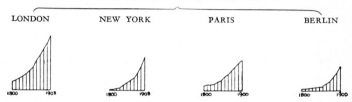

GROWTH OF POPULATION

LONDON   NEW YORK   PARIS   BERLIN

The GREAT CITY is a *recent* event, with devastating consequences !
The menace of to-morrow.

				1800	1880	1910
PARIS	.	.	.	647,000	2,200,000	3,000,000
LONDON	.	.	.	800,000	3,800,000	7,200,000
BERLIN	.	.	.	182,000	1,840,000	3,400,000
NEW YORK	.	.	.	60,000	2,800,000	4,500,000

VII

THE GREAT CITY

THE GREAT CITY IS A RECENT EVENT AND DATES BACK BARELY FIFTY YEARS

The growth of every great city has exceeded all prevision.

This growth has been a mad one, with disturbing possibilities.

The industrial life and the commercial life which are adjusting themselves to it are new phenomena on an overwhelming scale.

Means of transport are the basis of all modern activity.

The security of the dwelling is the condition of social equilibrium.

The new phenomenon of the great city has arisen within the framework of the old city.

The disproportion is such that an intense crisis has been brought about.

THIS CRISIS IS ONLY AT ITS BEGINNING. It is a constant source of disorder.

Such cities as do not adapt themselves quickly to the new conditions of modern life will be stifled and will perish. Other and better adapted cities will take their place.

The anachronistic persistence of the original skeleton of the city paralyzes its growth.

Industrial and commercial life will be stifled in towns which do not develop.

The conservative forces at work in great cities obstruct the development of transport, congest and devitalize activity, kill progress and discourage initiative.

The decayed state of these old towns and the intensity of modern toil lead to physical and nervous sickness. Modern life requires the recuperation of the forces which are used up in pursuit of it. Hygiene and moral health depend on the lay-out of cities. Without hygiene and moral health, the social cell becomes atrophied.

A country's worth can be measured by the vigour of its inhabitants.

The cities of to-day cannot respond to the demands of the life of to-day unless they are adapted to the new conditions.

The great cities determine the life of a country. If the great city is stifled, the country goes under.

In order to transform our cities we must discover the fundamental principles of modern town planning.

.(From a Manifesto accompanying the Diorama of a Contemporary City : Salon d'Automne, 1922.)

The great city determines everything : war, peace and toil. Great cities are the spiritual workshops in which the work of the world is done.

The solutions accepted in the great city are those which are singled out in the provinces ; fashions, styles, development of ideas and technical methods. That is the reason why the reorganization of the great city carries with it the renewal of the whole country.

Let us get down to facts : countries are composed of millions of individuals engaged on definite tasks ; the daily events of life are enough to preoccupy the restricted field of the day's thought. So it seems to us that we work as we do because this has always been the case. Yet history can show us alternations of famine and abundance, waves of happiness or of depression ; it shows us the rise of nations and hege-monies, and at the same time their decline and fall : it attributes different coefficients to different races as indications of their worth. The whole of history is an evolutionary movement. Born in the first place in the scattered tents of pastoral peoples, as mankind developed a social life so its field of action was transferred to villages and towns, and finally to the great capitals. These are now its home, and they affect profoundly the ordering of every other great city. Right away in the provinces, in factories or in ships at sea, in workshops and stores, in field and in wold, the work carried on is dictated by the great city : the conditions of this work, its quality, its price, its quantity and destination ; the demand and the means of execution all come from the great city.

Now that the machine age has let loose the consequences attaching to it, *progress has seized on a new set of implements with which to quicken its rhythm;* this it has done with such an intensification of speed and output that events have moved beyond our capacity to appreciate them ; and whereas mind has hitherto generally been in advance of accomplished fact, it is now, on the contrary, left behind by new facts whose acceleration continues without cease ; only similes can adequately describe the situation ; submersion, cataclysm, invasion. This rhythm has been accelerated to such a point that man— (who has after all created it with his small individual inventions, just as an immense conflagration can be started with a few pints of petrol and one little match)—man lives in a perpetual state of instability, insecurity, fatigue and accumulating delusions. Our physical and nervous organization is brutalized and battered by this torrent ; it makes its protest, of course, but it will soon give way unless some energetic decision, far-sighted and not too long delayed, brings order once more to a situation which is rapidly getting out of hand.

The peasant, as he works his land and sows his wheat, looks to the sun and rain to reveal once again the miraculous virtue of the seed. But other men, impelled by some force (the divine in man) to create with hand and mind, have laid the foundation stone of solidarity, and in getting away from mere individual achievement they are creating a collective manifestation. They are erecting an immense structure of labour. This collective manifestation is united by the spirit of " order," the first necessity of all action. A *feeling* is in the air, a sort of general assent to a group of new and opportune doctrines. The pyramid of values mounts slowly, stage by stage ; a succession of developments informed by a prophetical enthusiasm. Light streams about us on these heights. Beauty emerges at times, the result of a real harmony. New forms are constantly appearing, based on what pleases the senses and the spirit. From every corner those who feel the emptiness of the old narrow ways and the urge of ambition flock to these centres of activity. It is only quite recently that the available material means at our disposal have made it possible for a wealth of ambition to be tapped and directed

into the centres of our great cities. These centres grow overcrowded and spread ; men throng to them and squeeze in
somehow, only to have their wings scorched by a flame which
spares nobody. The law of survival operates perpetually
and with a recurring and brutal force. The great city, with

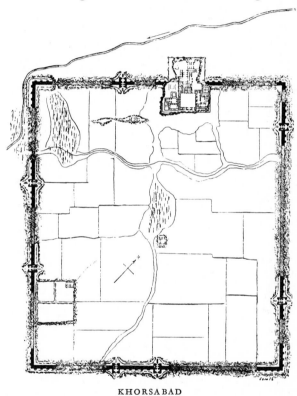

KHORSABAD

its throbbing and its tumult, crushes the weak and raises the
strong. And here it is, created by the peaceful *hinterlands*,
that we shall find the transcendental and intensely vital cell.

. . . And far away, another *hinterland* has created another
great city. And further away there are still others.

And these great cities challenge one another, for the mad
urge for supremacy is the very law of evolution itself to which

we are subjected. We challenge, we quarrel, we go to war.
Or else we agree and co-operate. From the great cities, the

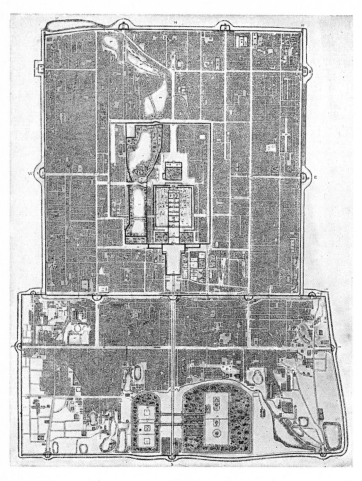

PEKIN

Compare this plan with that of Paris, a little further on. And we
Westerners felt called on to invade China in the cause of civilization !

living cells of the earth, come peace or war, abundance or
famine, glory, the triumph of the mind and beauty itself.

ROMAN CIVILISATION : AN AERIAL VIEW OF TIMGAD

NORTH AFRICA : KAIROUAN

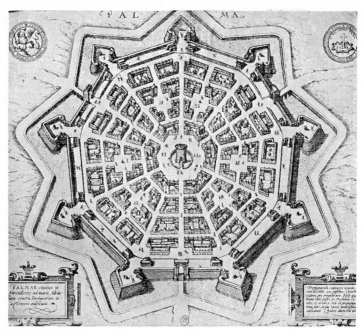

PALMANOVA : A FORTIFIED TOWN OF THE RENAISSANCE

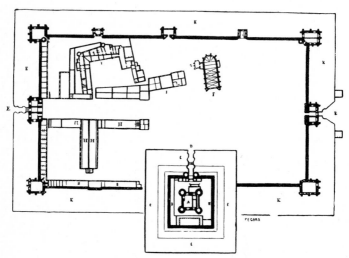

FRANCE : THE CHÂTEAU DE VINCENNES, FOURTEENTH CENTURY

The great city expresses man's power and might; the houses which shelter such an active ardour should follow a noteworthy plan. At least, this seems to my mind the logical conclusion of a quite simple reasoning.

Antiquity has left us, in its various remains, a demonstration of this fact. There have been golden moments when the power of the mind dominated the rabble. We have already seen it clearly in regard to Babylon and Pekin, and they are but examples among many; great cities and smaller ones, even quite small ones, which during certain noble periods were illumined by talent, science and experience. Everywhere

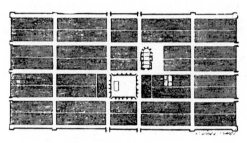

MONPAZIER (PÉRIGORD), TWELFTH CENTURY

there are remains, or units still intact, which provide us with a model: Egyptian temples, the rectilinear cities of North Africa (*e.g.* Kairouan), the sacred cities of India, the Roman cities of the Empire, or those built in the great tradition: Pompeii, Aigues-Mortes, Monpazier.

*

The structure of cities reveals two possibilities; a progressive growth, subject to chance, with resultant characteristics of slow accumulation and a gradual rise; once it has acquired its gravitational pull it becomes a centrifugal force of immense power, bringing the rush and the mob. Such was Rome; such are now Paris, London or Berlin.

Or on the other hand, the construction of a city as the

expression of a preconceived and predetermined plan embody-
ing the then known principles of the science ; such is Pekin
and such are the fortified cities of the Renaissance (*e.g.* Palmanova), or the colonial cities set by the Romans amongst
their barbarian subjects.

Our Western world, when Rome had been brought down

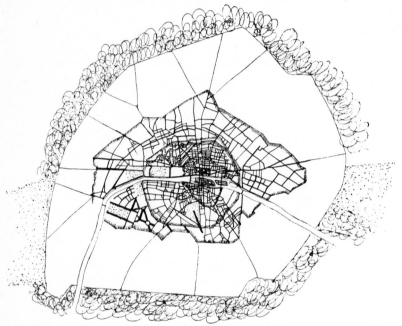

THE SIX SUCCESSIVE BOUNDARIES OF PARIS, DICTATED BY THE
" PACK-DONKEY'S WAY "

*On the periphery there is the strangle-hold of the nearer suburbs, except that
to right and left there are open spaces ; the Bois de Vincennes and the Bois
de Boulogne.*

exhausted by an effort too far-reaching, found itself left with
the most rudimentary equipment ; centuries passed before,
little by little, out of the entrenched camp (which was a
reminiscence of the savage surrounding his bivouac with his
wagons) there began to emerge an intention, a clear idea,
with a sufficiency of technical means to hand and with the

necessary provision in regard to financial resources. Men's minds, under great kings, formed their conception and strove to realize it ; there were magnificent attempts, rays of light amidst the barbaric stirring ; such are the Place des Vosges, under Louis XIII ; Versailles, and the Île Saint-Louis, under Louis XIV ; the Champ de Mars, under Louis XV ; l'Étoile and the main roads leading to Paris under Napoleon. And finally, that magnificent legacy left by a monarch to his people : the work of Haussmann under Napoleon III.

We struggle against chance, against disorder, against a policy of drift and against the idleness which brings death ; we strive for order, which can be achieved only by appealing to what is the fundamental basis on which our minds can work : geometry. In the general confusion there appear crystallizations of pure forms which bring strength and reassurance and give to beauty the material support it must have. At such moments, man has reflected well, he has employed the means proper to him and has produced works of a human order. So proud are we of his achievements that they form all our precedents. We surround these historic manifestations with such a veneration that it completely absorbs us. This pride is fully justified, but nevertheless we are apt to forget that we ourselves have so far done nothing. That living force, which inspired these noble creations, would be hated by us if by chance we met it to-day in the persons of men animated by similar passions. Our veneration creates in us a restless solicitude as if we were guarding the souls of the dead, as if we were watchmen in a cemetery. Our pre-occupation with the past has given us the soul of an under-taker's mute. And for all response to the splendid and over-whelming impact of this new age we take on the air of some old gentleman pottering about among his old engravings, who, completely taken aback, says, " Go away, I am *much* too busy ! "

So we may say that confusion is woven into the very texture of our modern cities. Built along the " Pack-Donkey's

Ways," [1] the childlike configuration of their beginnings has persisted without change in the very heart of the immense cities of to-day ; they are strangled in this fatal and disorderly network. This evil state of things grew worse from the tenth to the nineteenth century ; the Donkey's Ways have become institutions and the main arteries of the city. In those days death gave you a good run for your money. *But the age of machinery arose, and death knocks constantly at the door.*

In a mere hundred years the population of the great city has increased at an incredible rate.

	1800.	1880.	1910.
Paris	647,000	2,200,000	3,000,000
London	800,000	3,800,000	7,200,000
Berlin	182,000	1,840,000	3,400,000
New York	60,000	2,800,000	4,500,000

And when, after the War, the resources of our modern equipment were at last appreciated and more fully developed, then we began to feel choked. And this sense of suffocation is a real thing. We have had our warning.

All over the world the problem of the great city is one of tragic importance. Men of *business* have at last settled what environment best suits their affairs : they have now definitely concentrated in the centres of towns. The rhythm which actuates business is obvious ; it is speed and the struggle for speed. It is important to be housed close together and to be in touch ; important also to be able to act easily and quickly. Alas, we have become like the rusty engine of some out-of-date motor-car ; the chassis, the body, the seats (the peripheries of our cities) can carry on still, but the motor (the centre) is *seized !* This means complete breakdown. *The centres of the great cities are like an engine which is seized.* Here we have the very first problem of town planning.

A city which has come to a dead stop means a country which

[1] See Chapter I.

does the same. We hesitate to admit the truth to ourselves ; we have not the courage to diagnose the disease and recognize it, and to take the necessary bold measures to deal with it. Nevertheless, some forcible solution must be found.

But as against this there stand the following barriers :

The law of least resistance.

Lack of responsibility.

Respect for the past.

The curve of progress is quite clear : it is a matter of cause and effect, of deductions which are quite simple, consecutive and exact. But the dull and heavy mass of narrow interests, of acquired facts, of laziness, and of the sickly fog of a criminal sentimentality, raise up a giant obstacle. Boldly to confront this state of mind with the real facts is precisely the problem of town planning ; to animate with one common impulse the overwhelming complexity of the present social phenomenon and to maintain movement where paralysis has begun to set in.

*

Right up to the twentieth century, towns were laid out with a view to military defence. The boundary of a town was a definite thing, a clear organization of walls, gates with streets leading to them and from them to the centre.

Moreover, up to the nineteenth century a town was entered from the outside. To-day the city's gates are in its *centre*. For its real gates are the railway stations.

The city of to-day can no longer put up a military defence ; its boundaries have become a confused and stifling zone comparable only to a camp of roving gipsies, who may have plumped their overcrowded caravans down anywhere. The result is that the city can only extend through this formidable obstruction.

The new factor of suburbs immediately adjoining a town did not exist in the period of fortified towns whose sharply defined limits dictated the precise ordering of the town itself.

The centres of our towns are in a state of mortal sickness, their boundaries are gnawed at as though by vermin.

How to create a zone free for development is the second problem of town planning.

Therefore my settled opinion, which is quite a dispassionate one, is that the centres of our great cities must be pulled down and rebuilt, and that the wretched existing belts of suburbs must be abolished and carried farther out ; on their sites we must constitute, stage by stage, a protected and open zone, which when the day comes will give us absolute liberty of action, and in the meantime will furnish us with a cheap investment, whose value will increase tenfold, nay, a hundred-fold. If the centres of our cities have become a sort of intensely active form of capital for the mad speculation of private enterprise (New York is a typical instance), this pro-jected zone would represent a formidable financial reserve among the resources of municipalities.

Already in various countries municipalities are redeeming the suburban zones by expropriation. Actually it is a way of making sure of a " lung " for their city.

*

It is almost impossible to say everything and say it in a reasonable number of words. The theme is so new and its conclusions are so grave that, at the risk of repeating myself, it will perhaps be salutary to go into yet other aspects of the problem. Here, then, is an extract from a report made to the Town Planning Congress of Strasbourg in 1923.

Municipalities and the rulers of our great cities are busily engaged on the problems of the large suburbs, and are trying to provide housing further out for the popula-tions which have descended on our capital cities like an invasion; their efforts are praiseworthy but incomplete. They ignore the heart of the problem, which is that of the *centres of our great cities*. It is as though we were to concentrate on an athlete's muscles and blind ourselves to the fact that his heart was weak and his life in danger. If it is a good thing to take the overcrowded populations of the boroughs further out, it must also be remembered that every day, and at the same hour, those very same crowds which are better housed in the garden suburbs must return to the centre of the city. To improve housing conditions by the creation of garden cities is to leave entirely on one side the question of the city's *centre*.

We shall find it salutary to try and visualize exactly what is the phenomenon of the great city. The great city means simply four or five million individuals gathered together by chance in a definite spot. The great city has its *raison d'être*. In the biology of a country it is the vital organ; the whole national organization depends on it, and national organizations involve an international organization. The great city is the heart, the active centre of the cardiac system; it is the brain, the directing centre of the nervous system, and all its country's activities, all international events, are born in, and come from, the great city. Economics, sociology, politics, all are centred in the great city, and any modification it may bring about has its repercussion in the remotest corners of the provinces. The great city is the place where active " world elements " come together. This contact must be *immediate*, hand to hand; the decisions which arise from it are the result of hasty

THE ACTUAL DISPOSITION OF THE STREETS.

TRAFFIC MOVEMENT IN GREAT CITIES.

Ancient conditions still persisting.

Present conditions leading to the crisis which is only just beginning.

conferences and involve activities affecting all countries. The telegraph, the railway, the airplane have in less than fifty years so accelerated the speed at which international contacts can take place that a complete revolution has taken place in work. The march of ideas takes place all within the narrow area of the centres of great cities; these centres are, indeed, the vital cells of the world.

Now, the centres of our great cities to-day are, as it were, implements or tools which can only be utilized with the greatest difficulty; punctuality in keeping vital appointments is nearly impossible because of the crowded streets. More than that, the occupants of the offices in which all this business is done, these offices with their narrow corridors and dark rooms, suffer a real handicap, a real exhaustion as a result of so much congestion.

So the first conclusion we come to is that a harmful process of wear and tear—quite outside the conditions of their actual work—is rapidly affecting the very people who ought to be preserving all their mental alertness and powers of clear thinking; and that, furthermore, a country which had the centres of its towns well organized would have everything in its favour for gaining superiority over the others; an exactly similar superiority to that of the manufacturer who has an up-to-date plant. The results, good or bad, would be felt by the national purse.

It is necessary, therefore, to investigate with particular attention the present bad conditions in our great cities; it is a matter indeed of the greatest possible urgency. The lay-out of our great cities as we see them to-day shows that, as a result of their modest beginnings (the ancient small town or village) and the extraordinary developments of the last century, their centres are made up of short narrow lanes, and that only the periphery possesses anything like main arteries. Yet it is in the centre that the great and overwhelming circulation of traffic takes place, while the outskirts remain relatively empty, being given up to family life.

And if one compares the state of the streets of the great city with the state of its traffic, they will be seen to be wholly opposed to each other. The streets represent an old and out-of-date state of affairs; whilst traffic represents an existing state of affairs. Here is the crisis (there is no need for me to enlarge on this point; every great city is undergoing its disastrous effects). But if we look at the curve of the temperature chart in this crisis we must realize *that it is climbing madly;* we are getting into a blind alley.

INCREASE IN TRAFFIC.

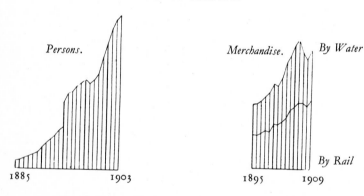

Persons.   Merchandise.   By Water

1885   1903   1895   1909   By Rail

Figures prove that the great city is a recent event, dating only some fifty years back; and that the increase in population has surpassed all anticipation. Between 1800 and 1910, that is to say, in one hundred years, Paris grew from 600,000 to 3,000,000 people; London from 800,000 to 7,000,000; Berlin from 180,000 to 3,500,000; New York from 60,000 to 4,500,000 : yet these cities are still living on their old buildings and lay-outs, which date from far before the astounding growth of population and of traffic (see the graphs above, whose curves show the increase of traffic from 1885 to 1905, both for ordinary traffic and transport of goods). The confusion is such that a growing anxiety is manifesting itself. The term " town planning " is of fairly recent date, and shows the germ of an idea. Quite naturally, the first efforts were directed to the least difficult problem—that of the suburb. A still more important point arises here; our present need is to reinvestigate the fundamental problems of the " dwelling " so that it can be made to answer the needs of a family life which has been entirely transformed by mechanism; the garden-city dwelling enables us to isolate the problem and experiment with it. Again, the law of least resistance, and the hardships entailed by the only possible remedies, lead us to ignore steadfastly the dreadful spectacle of the centres of our cities and the difficulty of doing anything with them; and strong-minded people tell us that we must move the centre somewhere else, we must build a new city, a new centre, far away, right beyond the suburbs; where it can be done comfortably, with no constraint and no pre-existing state of things. This is a pure fallacy. A centre is determined, it exists only because of what surrounds it; *its position is determined from a long way off* by innumerable convergings of every kind which it would be impossible to change; to shift the axle of a wheel means that you must move the whole wheel. As regards one of our great towns, you might as well set out to shift everything fifteen or twenty miles round about, which is altogether impossible. The axle of a wheel must remain fixed. In Paris, the axle has for a thousand years oscillated from left to right and right to left, between Notre Dame and the Place des Vosges, between the Place des Vosges and the Invalides, the Invalides and the Gare de l'Est, and between the Gare de l'Est and Saint Augustin. In relation to the wheel (*i.e.* the railways, the outskirts, the suburbs and the outer suburbs, the main arteries, the tubes and the tramways, the administrative and commercial centres,

TRAFFIC IN CAPITAL CITIES.

De-congest the centres.

the industrial zones and the residential quarters), this centre does not shift. *It has remained constant.*

It must still remain so. And, moreover, it is in itself immensely valuable, and forms a considerable slice of the national fortune, which would be wiped out at a word by any law that displaced it. To say, " It is quite simple, let us make a new centre at Saint-Germain-en-Laye," is to talk nonsense; it is like crying for the moon. It is a vacillation by means of which the stupid people who are always with us can gain a little more time. The centre must be modified in and about itself. It crumbles and rises up again through the ages; just as a man changes his skin each seven years and the tree its leaves year by year. We must concentrate on the centre of the city and change it, *which is after all the simplest solution, and more simply still the only solution.*

*

We are now in a position, therefore, to lay the foundations of modern town planning, based on four direct and concise requirements which are capable of meeting effectively the dangers which threaten us :

1. *We must de-congest the centres of cities* in order to provide for the demands of traffic.

2. *We must increase the density of the centres of cities* in order to bring about the close contact demanded by business.

3. *We must increase the means whereby traffic can circulate*, i.e. we must completely modify the present-day conception of the street, which has shown itself useless in regard to the new phenomenon of modern means of transport; tubes, motors, trams and airplanes.

4. *We must increase the area of green and open spaces ;* this is the only way to ensure the necessary degree of health and peace to enable men to meet the anxieties of work occasioned by the new speed at which business is carried on.

These four demands seem irreconcilable. Yet it would be well to realize how important they are, and how urgently necessary. And once the problem has been stated, town planning must find an answer. This it can do despite appearances. The technical apparatus and the organization of this age are such as to offer a satisfactory solution ; it is at this stage that the whole question becomes exciting, and that we can envisage the advent of a new age of grandeur and majesty. Architecture in the course of any particular evolution of a period marks its culminating point ; it is a consequence which is created by a whole mental outlook. Town planning is a support to architecture. A new architecture, *that can find its own full expression and no longer depends upon fancies*, is at hand. We are waiting for a form of town-planning that will give us freedom.

*

It may be worth while to consider the different kinds of inhabitants of a great city. As the seat of power (in the widest meaning of the word ; for in it there come together princes of affairs, captains of industry and finance, political leaders, great scientists, teachers, thinkers, the mouthpieces of the human soul, painters, poets and musicians), the city draws every ambition to itself : it is clothed in a dazzling mirage of unimaginable beauty ; the people swarm into it. Great men and our leaders install themselves in the city's centre. There too we find their subordinates of every grade, whose presence there at certain hours is essential, though their destinies are circumscribed within the narrower bounds of family life. The family is badly housed in the city. Garden cities satisfy these needs better. Finally, there is industry with its factories, thickly grouped, for various reasons, about the great centres : and working in these factories are multitudes of workers who can most satisfactorily be housed in garden cities.

So a classification of city dwellers would give us three main divisions of population : the citizens who live in the city ; the workers whose lives are passed half in the centre and half in the garden cities, and the great masses of workers who spend their lives between suburban factories and garden cities.

This classification gives us what is practically a programme for our town planning. And to put it into practice is to begin the simplification of the great cities. For they are, to-day, as a result of their intense growth, in a state of the most terrible chaos. Our programme of town planning might well be expressed thus in regard to a city of three million inhabitants : in the centre, but only for purposes of daily toil, there would be 500,000 to 800,000 people ; each evening the centre would be empty. The residential quarters of the city would absorb part, the garden cities the rest. Let us postulate then half a million citizens (round the centre) and two and a half millions in the garden cities.

The foregoing demonstration, which is clear as regards the principle, though the figures may vary, demands an ordered solution. It lays down for us the main lines of modern town planning, it settles for us the proportions of the city as regards the relationship between its centre and the residential districts, and puts before us the problem of means of communication and transport. It suggests a basis for urban hygiene, for methods of housing, for the lay-out of the streets and the particular forms of these; it dictates the relative densities and consequently the actual mode of construction of the city's centre, its residential quarters and its garden cities.

*

The question of sky-scrapers preoccupies Europe. In Holland, in England, in Germany, France and Italy the first theoretical essays have been made. But the sky-scraper cannot be isolated from the question of the streets and of transport both horizontal and vertical.

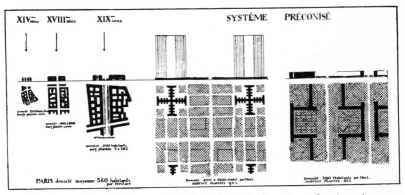

These plans are all to the same scale, and give the dimensions of various sites built over and of streets in the fourteenth, eighteenth and nineteenth centuries (Gothic, Louis XV, Napoleon III). In the centre is a suggestion for a modern site, densely populated, i.e. a sky-scraper of sixty storeys (5 per cent. of the surface built upon, 95 per cent. planted over). Also a housing scheme with " set-backs " (15 per cent. of the surface built upon, 85 per cent. planted over ; no internal courtyards, and immense open spaces).

Family life, therefore, will be definitely banished from the centre of our city. It seems most probable, as things are, that the sky-scraper cannot adequately provide for family life; for its internal economy demands so elaborate a system that if one of these structures is to pay, only business can afford the cost : while the means of getting about in what is practically a series of superimposed stations is so elaborate that it could never be appropriate to family life.

The residential quarters of the city would undergo the same rational transformation. The principal roads, their axes set at roughly 400-yard intervals, would cut through them. And, contrary to age-long custom, the buildings would not be grouped in great rectangular blocks overhanging the streets and subdivided in their interior into numerous wells and courtyards. Under a system of building with setbacks,[1] doing away completely with internal courtyards, the housing blocks

---

[1] This word is perhaps a trifle ambiguous. The plan of these buildings would follow the line of battlements laid horizontally. The French is " à redents."—F. E.

would be set at distances of 200, 400 or 600 yards in parks larger than the Tuileries. The town would, in fact, be one immense park; 15 per cent. of it would be built over, and all the rest planted; yet it would have a density of population equal to that of the congested Paris of to-day. Main axial roads fifty yards wide would cut across each other at not less than 400 yards distance, for modern motor traffic demands the suppression of two-thirds of the existing streets: there would be parks for sport and pleasure contiguous to the dwellings, all internal courtyards would be suppressed, there would be a radical transformation of the appearance of the city and an architectural contribution of the greatest importance.

If only the question is minutely studied in the light of reason, and is touched with some poetical feeling, the replanning of a great city should give results which are as practical as they are eminently architectural. The solutions of the problem which it can bring about take their rise from the purely theoretical analysis of the problem; of course they are bound to upset all our accustomed habits. But have not our very existences become completely changed within the last few years? Mankind thinks in terms of theory and acquires thereby certain theoretical certitudes. Theory suggests a line of conduct; and if he feels himself securely established in his first principles, man is able to embark on problems of a practical nature.

*

So many problems are raised by the question of town planning; so many interesting considerations and points of a technical or sentimental kind, that it seems to me advisable at this point to set forth the scope of this inquiry.

Beginning with "The Donkey's Way and Man's Way," the problem was shown as arising out of a most urgent actual situation. But immediately we attempt to follow the dictates of reason in order to escape from some evil pass, our hearts begin their counter-chorus. To assure ourselves against every risk, one primordial human basis is needed: "Order." And then, to appease our sensibilities and delicacies, we have "Sensibility comes into Play" and "Permanence." But here the æsthete comes in with his fears and alarms, for he is often a nuisance; in order to set him on a solid, human and well-chosen basis, we have "Classification and Choice (A Survey)" and "Classification and Choice (Timely Decisions)." For to-day, we have "The Great City." Then we have bald facts: "Statistics." Prognostications in the chapter headed "Newspaper Cuttings"; and acquired facts in "Our Technical Equipment." Then a definite and concrete proposal for a modern town-planning scheme supported by actual plans: in "A Contemporary City," followed by a pathetic case of to-day : " Paris and its Centre." In order to present this pathetic case fully we have an inquiry into history : " Physic or Surgery." And to support all my arguments and inspire enthusiasm in view of the approaching realization of a form of town planning worthy of the twentieth century we have " Finance." And to conclude with the contemporary situation, where enterprise, courage and far-sightedness strive with apathy, fear and confusion we have " Discordant Noise." [1]

Thus it may be that some of my readers, trusting to cold reason and their warm feelings, may find in these pages something to stimulate the generous powers of their imaginations.

---

[1] In the end I had to leave out this chapter. It was too painful and there was no room for it. In any case, it was too depressing. Alas ! I have plenty of matter for it which is at the disposition of anybody with a sense of humour !

Statistics show us the past and foreshadow the future; they provide us with the necessary figures and interpret our graphs and curves. Statistics help to formulate the problem.

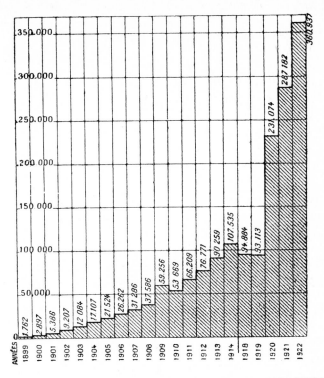

FIG. I.—GRAPH SHOWING THE INCREASE IN MECHANICAL
TRANSPORT IN FRANCE DURING THE YEARS 1899–1922

VIII

STATISTICS

A : B = A¹ : B¹

STATISTICS are the Pegasus of the town planner. They
are tedious things, meticulous, passionless and impassive.
All the same they are a jumping-off ground for poetry, the base
from which the poet may leap into the future and the unknown,
although his feet remain planted on the solid groundwork of
figures, graphs, the eternal verities. Actually his lyricism will

have its interest for us, since it speaks our language, treats of what interests us, and quickens us in the direction in which we are moving, presenting us with those solutions only which are appropriate to our requirements.

Statistics give us an exact picture of our present state and also of former states ; connecting them with a line so expressive that the past speaks clearly to us, so that by following the development of the curve we are enabled to penetrate into the future and make those truths our own which otherwise we could only have guessed at. Thus the poet pursues his way through a number of vital truths which are indispensable to the sure performance of the work that lies before us.

By virtue of statistics we can achieve an almost instantaneous grasp of a problem of whose complexities we are altogether ignorant ; and thus choose a sure path towards fresh creations. Confronted by complexities, people go under ; some individuals are always liable to this, but there are others, rarer ones, who are never in any danger. Town planning is indeed a stormy sea in which people go under. The first stroke, the first dive makes one feel that one is drowning, so violently is one assailed by the multitude of waves and their deafening noises, one is lucky if one can but grasp at the safeguard of conscientiousness and care in one's work, which is, after all, only the conscientiousness and care of a horse in blinkers between the shafts.

Under such dangerous conditions as regards the future there is being slowly pursued the long-drawn-out task whose aim is to organize our cities, to police and discipline them, to keep them efficient for production, and lift them out of the chaos which stifles them. A gigantic task carried on by the municipal services, which are always criticized and never praised, because they are like the policeman who, during public celebrations, never ceases restraining our outbursts, and directing the crowd, in that eternal and irritating way that seems peculiar to policemen. The conscientious and careful people who make statistics have become what they are through meticulous toil ; their minds have become shaped in the unchangeable mould of the worker in mosaic or the expert weaver, bending over his thousand tiny stones or innumerable threads of wool ; a spirit of analysis and not of invention, a spirit which is so deadened by constantly dealing with small special cases that it becomes incapable of conceiving any sort of clear and open, bold or inspired idea.

Let us be just to these men of good-will and honest conscience. Their willingness is immense and their dull and long-continued labours are a source of great strength. Humble enough in their individual capacity, like the soldier on the field of battle, united together they make an army : their lot is cast amid din and confusion ; with an over-precise gift of analysis, their tragedy is that they are asked to create. Concentrated though they are upon these almost insoluble urban problems, they are not the persons of whom we can demand those tremendous strides through which the course of events can be directed. They merely make statistics. And statistics are a raw material. No one can ask a raw material to turn itself into a finished product. It needs a practical workman to convert raw materials.

The public has little notion of what the administration of a great city involves, with its many and varied departments : no one has any idea of the tremendous mechanism of the great city, which keeps four million people, each of whom is actuated by his own individual and ungoverned passions, in a state of discipline—four million people who want to live in accordance with their own free wills, each claiming to live his own life, although such a claim creates a state of dramatic and exasperated tension.

Nevertheless this tension follows always those hidden currents by which the masses are slowly but surely led ; slowly yet sometimes contrarily, at the cost of violence and disorder. To recognize the presence of these currents, to measure their force and apprehend their direction is the job of the statistician.

I have seen these modest specialists in meticulosity at work. The encounter, coming in the midst of this inquiry, might well have made me almost giddy at the thought of all this mechanism whose interlocking parts have been multiplied and subdivided so that they might engage more closely and more delicately. I felt that when one is in direct contact with a *mechanism*, the idea of even a minute change is terrifying ; you hear something give in advance and you foresee a breakdown. And one becomes respectful and timid. Personal desires are pushed into the background. It is a dangerous thing to get into too close contact with the machine if you want to attempt anything. And I perceived the sort of insult to the *particular truth of the moment* which every proposal to modify the urban system must be, and I was able to understand why such genuine indignation has been aroused when sometimes I have given utterance to some new conception. I have said enough ; nothing of any value can come out of a world so hopelessly caught in this complicated machinery which is so inextricably locked. Any important advance can come only from without, from a quarter where no question at all arises of such a thing as inextricably locked machinery. Statistics are one of the results of these complications. Let us leave them alone, for the time has come to destroy what cannot be mended ; only so can we be saved. We must be remorseless. More than that, we must free ourselves from the complications of the machine, so that our conceptions may be as straightforward and simple as those of a child. As I said to one of the most active of those who are fighting the machine : [1] " I mean to keep outside all these petty established facts ; I refuse to interest myself in the struggle between the various interests ; all I want, making full use of your statistics, is to work out in an unbiassed frame of mind a conception of the future which shall be rational and simple, a thing both of utility and of beauty ; my aim is to search

[1] M. Émile Massard, President of the second Commission of the Municipal Council of Paris.

for pure governing principles, to isolate the problem from particular examples, and in this way to arrive at the fundamental principles of modern town planning. Once these principles are established as sure facts, anybody can then take his own example ; Paris, for instance." [1]

*

THE MOVEMENT OF POPULATION

The population of a great city which has grown from 500,000 to 4,000,000 follows a curve of growth which increases more and more violently. The curve would go on to infinity but

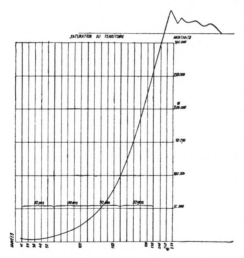

FIG. 2—GENERAL CURVE OF THE GROWTH OF POPULATION

The main spaces indicate periods of fifty years, and it will be seen at what a constantly increasing rate the growth has taken place.

[1] I have recently read the report of the Municipal Council of Paris as presented by M. É. Massard in 1923 on behalf of the second Commission. It deals with the problem of traffic in the great cities. In every country we find a solid phalanx of proposals in regard to this desperate situation, but these proposals are nothing more than a further complication of the infernal " machine." It cannot be done; the result would be a complete impasse. There is a complete lack of any constructive proposal : it becomes a stampede.

for the fact that it reaches a point where it begins to slow down, at the moment when the country around the great city has reached its maximum birth-rate. The city's population may climb from 1 to 2, 3, 4, 5, 6 or 7 millions with an acceleration uniform with the curve of its earlier growth. For practical purposes we may consider this increase as unlimited.

If we study the curve of growth in a district or suburb, it will be seen that it is of precisely the same nature as that of the great city; it is a simultaneous phenomenon. None the less, in the case of a district there occurs a " stop " : *i.e.* the moment where the capacity of the district is definitely limited by its superficial area (whereas the superficial area of a great city is capable of infinite extension). At this point we have super-saturation, a population in excess of the district's normal

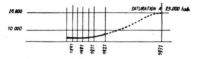

FIG. 3.—LE BOURGET, A SUBURB OF PARIS OF RECENT GROWTH

capacity, overcrowding and a crisis in housing; and finally, as the pendulum swings first one way and then another, we reach a settled condition of full saturation. This will continue until some new external event intervenes, such as a modification in building methods, necessitating amendments in the laws relating to structures; for instance, we may some day be permitted to build to a height of twenty storeys instead of to the six or seven at present decreed by law. (Fig. 2.)

The Department which deals with the growth of Paris has in this way worked out a curve of growth for each district in the Department of the Seine. These curves enable us from now on to foresee what a similar district will be like in fifty years' time, and therefore to plan a lay-out of streets, parks, cemeteries, public services, etc. which shall be adequate to such a growth.

Statistics enable us to formulate our problem.

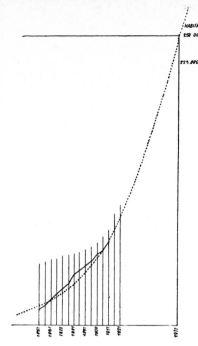

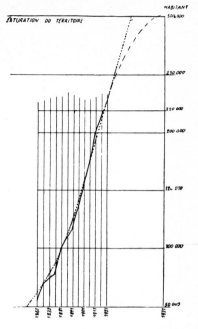

FIG. 4.—SAINT DENIS, A PARIS SUBURB

showing its growth, which is in full swing.

FIG. 5.—PARIS, THE 15TH ARRONDISSEMENT

A growth nearing its limit (actually determined by the laws relating to the height of buildings).

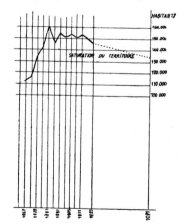

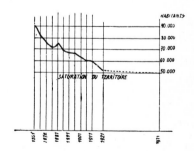

FIG. 6.—PARIS, THE 10TH ARRONDISSEMENT.

A growth surpassing its capacity (under existing conditions).

FIG. 7.—PARIS, THE 1ST ARRONDISSEMENT.

A growth returning to its normal level owing to the migration of the inhabitants.

These five curves, 3, 4, 5, 6 and 7, placed end to end, would give the graph of general development shown in Fig. 2 on page 111.

BUSINESS INEVITABLY GRAVITATES TOWARDS THE CENTRES OF GREAT CITIES

Where is the proof of this ? We find it in Statistics, which can even tell us exactly where and with what intensity such developments take place.

FIG. 8.—DENSITY OF POPULATION. DEPARTMENT OF THE SEINE.
PARIS SUBURBS (ACCORDING TO THE CENSUS OF 1911 AND 1921)

" A " shows the exodus of city dwellers, and replacement by business. (A striking demonstration of how business centres can spring up in ten years.)
" B " shows the afflux into the suburbs. (The same phenomenon affects the whole department.)

The diagram in Fig. 8 shows clearly the increase and decrease in resident population in the Department of the Seine according to the census. It shows that a large number of districts have been completely transformed, in that the inhabitants have moved further out and the houses have been turned into suites of offices.

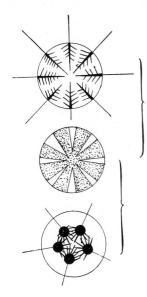

Direction of traffic before the creation of railways

The state of the arteries of circulation at that time.

To-day a similar state of things exists.

But the creation of railway stations has precipitated the crowds into the smallest possible area and among the narrowest streets.

FIG. 9.

In the Department which deals with the growth of Paris can be found a diagram giving the density of population per hectare.[1] The dark patches represent the most thickly populated quarters, and it is a significant fact that in the diagram which deals with the incidence of tuberculosis we find these very same overcrowded quarters marked dark also. The moral is easily drawn ; we must call in the house-breaker ; we shall have no difficulty in indicating the quarters which must be pulled down. Other diagrams will show where to rebuild.

[1] About two and a half acres.—F. E.

THE GREAT CITY OF TO-DAY IS DESTROYING ITSELF

The great city is born of the railway. In the past the city was entered by gates in the ramparts ; traffic, both on wheels and on foot, split up and was dissipated on the way to the town's centre. There was no particular reason for congestion at the centre. But the railway led to the construction of stations right in the heart of great cities. Now, these centres are generally formed of a network of extremely narrow streets. Into these narrow streets crowds are precipitated by the railways. The suggestion has often been made that the railway stations should be transferred to the outskirts. But statistics negative this proposition. Business demands that hundreds of thousands of travellers must at 9 a.m. find themselves right in the very heart of the city where business is carried on. Statistics show us that business is conducted in the centre. This means that wide avenues must be driven through the centres of our towns. *Therefore the existing centres must come down.* To save itself, every great city must rebuild its centre.

BUSINESS DEMANDS THE GREATEST POSSIBLE SPEED IN REGARD TO TRAFFIC

The automobile has created business, and business is constantly developing the automobile, and no limit to this development can so far be seen.[1]

In Paris, according to M. Massard, the combined superficial area of the vehicles using the roads is actually greater than that of the roads themselves. Fig. 10 gives a graph of the actual superficial area available to traffic in the form of

[1] M. Massard, in the report I have already referred to, reiterates again and again that " *speed is the very epitome of modern society,*" and this conviction governed all the debates at the International Conference on Traffic held at Seville in 1923.

roads, and of the combined superficial area of the vehicles using these roads. Where do all these motors go ? To the centre. But there is no proper superficial area available for traffic in the centre.

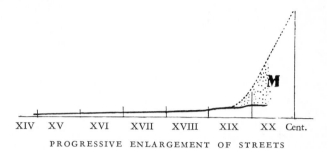

PROGRESSIVE ENLARGEMENT OF STREETS

Fig. 10.—The dotted zone M *shows to what extent the provision of streets should have developed. Unfortunately we are a long way from this. Hence the present crisis.*

It will have to be created. The existing centres must come down.

Fig. 1 at the head of this chapter gives a graph of the

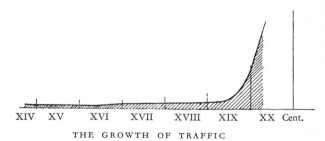

THE GROWTH OF TRAFFIC

Fig. 11.—The twentieth century marks a violent break from a long-established state of things. The development of the curve leads to a state of things absolutely unforeseen.

increase in motor traffic during the last twenty-three years in France. The diagram does not include the years 1923 and 1924, but the rate of increase in these years was much greater than in 1921 and 1922. Motor traffic is a new factor which will inevitably have far-reaching consequences for the great city. Our towns were totally unadapted for it. With the result that in New York, for example, the congestion is so complete that business men have to leave their cars on the outskirts of the town and take the tube to their offices. This is a striking and paradoxical state of affairs.

In Fig. 12 the diagram shows the rate of increase in automobile production in the United States during the years 1912

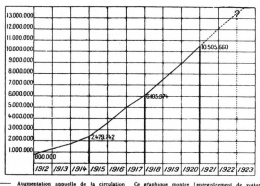

FIG. 12.—ANNUAL INCREASE IN THE PRODUCTION OF MOTOR-CARS AS SHOWN BY FIGURES PUBLISHED IN 1922

The record does not go further back than 1912.

to 1921. The graph is a striking diagonal which gets steeper with each year.

I give in Fig. 13 a table of figures which shows how the tide is rising. This table, again, does not include the years 1923 and 1924, and *these were years which saw the revival of industrial activity.*

The centre of the great city is like a funnel into which every street shoots its traffic. The map of the Public Transport Services of Paris shows many and multiple lines in its centre which represent the tram and 'bus routes (Fig. 14). This map should also show, in the same critical places, black patches to

	Carrefour Rivoli-Sébastopol	Carrefour Drouot	Champs Elysées-Ch. de Marly	Carrefour Royale-St-Honoré	TOTALS
1908 3–9 February	33,993	57,409	45,710	69,228	206,340
1910 18–24 April	37,528	60,711	74,237	73,178	242,654
1912 13–19 May	42,681	51,289	81,437	85,557	260,964
1914 27 April–3 May	62,703	56,174	88,707	83,410	290,102
1919 19–25 February 26 May–4 June	34,436 40,355	44,772 54,764	66,440 114,368	65,081 84,408	210,729 293,895
1920 3–4 November	48,805	60,978	90,143	82,944	282,870
1921 30 May–5 June	50,702	65,970	100,656	81,174	298,302
1922 15 to 21 March	48,641	65,107	104,862	88,351	306,961

FIG. 13.—OFFICIAL FIGURES SHOWING THE NUMBERS OF MOTOR-CARS PASSING AT VARIOUS MAIN CROSSINGS IN PARIS

represent general motor traffic. And all the time, below ground, the tubes are discharging their millions of travellers each day.

Now, all modern motor vehicles are constructed for speed. But in the actual state of our streets, a further diagram proves that the highest speed obtainable by motors in the city of to-day is about ten miles an hour ! ! ! The motor factories (national industries) struggle hard to attain speeds of sixty

miles an hour and over, but the existing conditions in our
towns keep us down, perforce, to ten miles an hour !

For the forms of our streets are not adapted to modern
traffic. Most of them date from the sixteenth and seventeenth
centuries. Remember that in the middle of the sixteenth
century the only wheeled traffic in Paris consisted of *two*

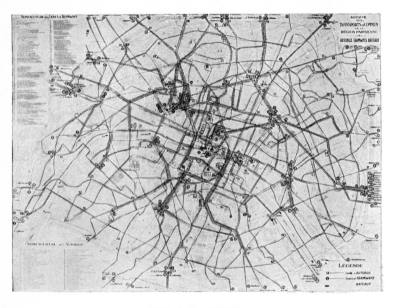

FIG. 14.—PARIS.

A map showing the tram and omnibus systems.

vehicles, the Queen's coach and that of the Princess Diane.
The nineteenth and twentieth-century street is adapted for
horse-drawn vehicles only.

In whatever direction one looks there is everywhere
congestion.

Where do all the thousands of cars in the modern city
pull up to park ? By the curb, hindering other traffic ; traffic
killing traffic, in fact. The New York business man leaves

PARIS. — La Place du Palais-Royal.

PARIS. — La Place de la Concorde.

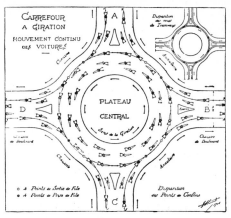

HÉNARD'S SCHEME OF 1906 FOR GYRATORY TRAFFIC OR A
" MERRY-GO-ROUND "

*He had only horse-drawn traffic in mind! The two picture post-cards above
show that in 1909 there were hardly any motor-cars on the streets. They
provide a striking indication of the rate at which the evolution of motor traffic
has come about.*

his car in the suburbs. We must create vast and sheltered public parking places where cars can be left during working hours.

The streets of to-day are useless for this purpose. The corridor-street has had its day ; there are a thousand reasons why. We must create another type of street.

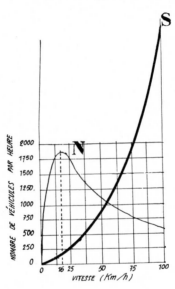

The curve N shows the maximum point of traffic and its speed (1775 vehicles travelling at ten miles an hour). If the rate of speed were sixty miles an hour the street could only take 500 cars an hour. This curve is based on the principle that every car must have room enough to pull up quickly in case of necessity. If overhead tracks for fast traffic, and with few intersections, were constructed above the ordinary streets, then instead of the curve N we should have the curve S ; that is to say, the capacity to take traffic would be in direct relation to the vastly increased rate of motion.

If we ask ourselves how the new type of street is to be determined, we must first examine the statistics relating to the volume and direction of traffic as far as it concerns heavy vehicles (*i.e.* vans and lorries) : this will give us, as it were, the beds of these slow and powerful streams of traffic.

We must then work out the figures in relation to the cost

of putting in drains, mains for water, gas and electricity, the telephone, compressed air, and so on ; and of the annual maintenance of these vital organs which are now placed in the most dangerous sectors of the city !

And, finally, the cost of the excavation and clearing involved in rebuilding over the area of these same sectors. Having got thus far, we may well reflect a little and make it quite clear to ourselves that the enormous superficial area of such a town as Paris has been excavated to a depth of over twelve feet for the purpose of constructing basements in a humid and unhealthy soil at an incredible cost ; and that this immense buried area of masonry is practically useless. We shall come to the conclusion that it is utterly useless nowadays to excavate under a house, since concrete piles suffice for foundation. And from the fact that the street is no longer a track for cattle, *but a machine for traffic, an apparatus for its circulation*, a new organ, a construction in itself and of the utmost importance, a sort of extended workshop, we shall conclude that it must have more than one storey, and that it would be possible, merely by the exercise of common-sense, for towns built on piles to materialize ; this would be a simple solution of our problem, and could be carried out at any time we wished. And statistics, again and again, will confirm our conclusions.

This is only an example.

*

And, finally, other statistics are needed (possibly they exist) which will give us a basis for our attempts to stir to action the world . . . of officialdom :

"*He stamped his hoof, and from the mount of Helicon Pegasus caused to pour forth that spring of Hippocrene from which it is said the poet draws his inspiration.*"

In order to gain a true conception of the real street of to-day we must put these questions to ourselves :

1. What, at the rush hours, are the numbers of travellers from the suburbs disgorged at each station ?

2. At what rate do the trees which border our present streets wither and die, as a result of the gases given off by petrol and burnt oil or of the radiation of heat from the narrow canyons formed by our streets and their houses in their present deplorable relationship ? [1]

3. What sort of curve would the nervous system of an inhabitant of the great city show during, say, the last ten years ? And his respiratory system ?

In order that our towns may be freed from the existing congestion and a vastly increased superficial area, under thoroughly healthy conditions, be added to them we will ask ourselves this question :

What would be the increase in the superficial area of towns by the use of flat roofs and terraces, water-tight and accessible, on all buildings ? For some day our ever-present reactionaries may see the permanent adoption of this form of building, which merely follows the dictates of common-sense, and makes use of modern methods ; when this happens, town planning will be able to extend its operations to THE ROOF of the city, bringing in a portion of this accessible surface and forming there a new system of quiet and peaceful streets, far from noise and surrounded by trees.

In order that those who, in the near future, will have to carry out these ideas may have the necessary financial means at their disposal, we ask this question :

How are the site values of a city to be reckoned :

(*a*) When business has invaded a district and has pushed out the middle-class resident ?

(*b*) When blocks of old buildings or slums are de-

---

[1] " Up to the end of the War Paris was a city of shady avenues. It is now a city of streets congested with motor traffic and bordered with stark trunks, from which a few shrivelled leaves flutter down on to the asphalt." *The Evening Standard*, Nov. 3, 1927.—F. E.

molished and new and wide arteries driven through their sites ?

Etc., etc.

*

Statistics show us the past and foreshadow the future ; they provide us with the necessary figures and interpret our graphs and curves.

In other ways these new factors (that is to say, the nineteenth century with its railways, its motor traction, its telegraphic and telephonic communication and so on) have totally upset the even course of events.

If A = the ancient roads,

If B = the ancient population plus its needs in regard to traffic (both of people and goods), its hygiene, morale, etc.,

If A^1 = the new roads,

If B^1 = the present-day population, its needs in regard to traffic (both of people and goods), its hygiene, morale, etc.,

The equation then becomes :

$A : B = A^1 : B^1$.

A and B were proportionate to each other.

A^1 is still practically the same as A, therefore $A = A^1$.

B has increased enormously.

The equation therefore becomes absurd : $A : B = A : B^1$.

We can show it thus :

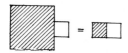

The products of the means and of the extremes give :

Which is absurd.

The great city of to-day as it exists in actuality is an absurdity.

*

But, in actual fact, it is using up and slowly wearing out millions of human beings ; and the surrounding country on which it feeds is doomed to decay.

Statistics are merciless things.

" Young man, 29, with serious intentions, no friends, desires to make the acquaintance of a really nice shop-girl with a view to marriage. Great capacity for devotion. Write J. R. . . . . . ."

HEARTRENDING FAREWELLS OF THE FATHER OF A FAMILY ABOUT
TO CROSS THE STREET IN FRONT OF THE GARE DE L'EST
Le Journal (Cartoon by Capy).

IX

NEWSPAPER CUTTINGS AND CATCHWORDS

TRANSLATOR'S NOTE.—This chapter, in the original French edition, consisted largely of cuttings from French newspapers. Most of these, referring to traffic problems, street accidents, housing and town planning, are mainly applicable to the local problems of Paris. It would have been a simple matter to include similar cuttings from English newspapers, but Le Corbusier's text here given sufficiently explains the points in question, and it was thought better to include instead an important analysis of various widespread objections to his scheme—an analysis first published by Le Corbusier in the *Almanach d'Architecture Moderne,* 1925.

In three instances it seemed only kind to include, for the reader's delectation, the original cuttings.—F. E.

NEWSPAPER CUTTINGS

I ONLY look at one newspaper a day, and yet . . . !
Newspapers give us the curve registered by that seismograph the world; their news paragraphs emphasize the daily drama which is being enacted all around us, and the workings of science, history, economics and politics.

Town planning has now been for some years a question of the day.   It has become a sort of dumping ground for every difficult and unresolved problem such as the birth-rate, the social equilibrium, alcoholism, crime, the morale of the great city, civic affairs and so forth.   *Urbi et orbi, within and without the city*, this is the time-worn phrase which indicates the immense power of the city, that without the city there is nothing. In fact town planning is the expression and result of that social contract by means of which the collective existence of mankind has been made possible.

And latterly, also, town planning has come to take a more and more important place in the crowded columns of our newspapers.

The interest of newspaper cuttings lies partly in the fact that even a modest line may reveal as much as the headlines of the leading articles.   The newspaper registers temperature, and that of the great city is at fever point.

*

Town planning will soon no longer be a vague and un-resolved problem, it is bound to become one of the burning questions of the day.   We shall not be able to ignore much longer the daily problems which face us in this connection.

TRAFFIC PROBLEMS

I give below a few typical headlines. . . .
"WE MUST LEARN TO CIRCULATE."
" TRAFFIC ON THE BRAIN."
" TOWN PLANNING."
" THE AVOIDANCE OF TRAFFIC CONGESTION."
" THE MULTIPLICATION OF POLICEMEN."
" ONE HORSE CAN HOLD UP MOTORS AGGREGATING 1,000 H.P."
After fifty years of this age of machinery we have arrived at the internal combustion engine.   Speed has increased thirty-

fold. The factories turn out numberless motor-cars, and everybody wants one in order to get about quickly, for speed is now a prime necessity.

The street of 400 years ago, or even of 4,000 years ago, still exists, but it no longer has any meaning for us.

The city is congested and bottled up, and the newspapers register the increasing volume of our protests—and of our difficulties.

STREET ACCIDENTS

The cutting given on p. 134 will suffice for this subject. There is the same wretched story every day, for in every newspaper edition we have the curt mention of deaths and bad accidents.

THE STREET

The street is a traffic machine ; it is in reality a sort of factory for producing speed traffic. The modern street is a new " organ." We must create a type of street which shall be as well equipped in its way as a factory.

If once we consider seriously the problem of the street and arrive at a solution, our existing great cities will be shaken to their foundations, and the Age of Town Planning on a noble scale will have begun.

When we find the President of the second Traffic Commission of the Paris Municipal Council basing all his researches on the " factor of speed which must be safeguarded at all costs," then we can say that such a profession of faith is a programme, and that such a programme is a profession of faith.

We have seen practically every horse cleared off the streets of Paris, but the motor is still thought of as a luxury. But if we consider the important part played in our urban existence by the motor lorry, we shall see that we must devise streets which take the motor lorry into account.

THE CONSEQUENCES

Here are a few more headings. . . .

" THE TREES IN OUR STREETS ARE PERISHING."

" THE DRAMA OF THE HOUSING QUESTION."

" *PARIS-FLIRT*."

" THE PRESS GROWS ANXIOUS."

First of all we have a simple and objective result from these conditions : the trees are dying ! And what about the inhabitants ?

Paris-Flirt, which is a comic paper, can furnish some indication of the loneliness and unhappiness of human beings who are forced to exist without a normal social life, who emerge from the tube, from their offices or their workshop, to find themselves completely alone and cut off from human relationships.[1]

The Press is troubled at the absence of a town-planning scheme which may ameliorate to some extent the conditions under which so many live and may appease their discontent.

Here we have the physical menace and the moral disorder of the great city.

WHAT IS TO BE DONE ?

Where there's a will there's a way. This was the good old maxim my mother taught me.

A PROGRAMME

Any progress must depend on a well-thought-out programme.

Now a programme can be of two kinds : a tinkering fragmentary affair, or one which is adequate. Everyone who has a glimmering of a solution to these problems should put forward his ideas. Events march swiftly, and a new age is replacing an epoch that is dead and gone. Our schemes must

[1] See the half-title to this chapter.

be worked out by the new generation. Progress is so over-whelming and the programmes put forward are so limited and lacking in foresight. But we can never have too many of them. In a very few years' time town planning will have affected so many interests that a large part of technical and industrial activity will be devoted to it.

And so it is that the newspapers are forced every day to include in their crowded columns this question of town planning, a question on which our very existence depends.

CATCHWORDS

" *Is the next generation really destined to pass its existence in these immense geometrical barracks, living in standardized mass-production houses with mass-production furniture; conveyed at the same hours by the same trains to the same sky-scrapers into identically similar offices? Their games, and by that I mean their recreations, are all based on the same model; every one will have his little piece of ground, and if any one is fond of gardening, here are the garden plots; we may note that the individual watering-can is forbidden, as being out of date and not over-efficient; for even down to the least important of pleasurable occupations we must think of efficiency. Poor creatures! what will they become in the midst of all this dreadful speed, this organization, this terrible uniformity? So much logic taken to its extreme limits, so much ' science,' so much of the ' mechanical' everywhere present and challenging one on every page and claiming its insolent triumph on every possible occasion—here is enough to disgust one for ever with ' standardization ' and to make one long for ' disorder.' "*

(*L'Architecte*, Paris, September, 1925.)

This criticism in regard to the present volume appeared in *L'Architecte*, a journal which is to be found in every French architect's office. The article of which it forms a part was written in an appreciative and even flattering spirit. This extract may be taken to represent the plaintive attitude of a whole generation. The attitude is largely governed by worn-out phrases and old catchwords; let us analyze this very " standardized " protest, phrase by phrase. . . .

These immense geometrical barracks are designed to introduce a quite new variety into the urban scene, and to replace the " corridor-street " as it exists in every large town by noble

LE PIÉTON FAUTIF —Comment voulez-vous que je lui flanque une contravention? Il manque la partie où sont ses papiers!

Le Journal, December 16, 1924.

architectural perspectives, through the play and interplay of projections and recessions, " set-backs," cellular constructions and the great sky-scrapers. If anyone will examine carefully my plan for a Contemporary City, and imagine that he is taking a walk through the town and keeping in mind the great increase in height of the buildings, he will see that *the scene changes with each step* and is never repeated; that the " corridor-street " is gone and is replaced by a scheme where space and an infinite architectural variety are possible.

Mass-production houses: quite naturally so, as in the case of any other period where a " style " and a definite type of urban dwelling have been achieved, as in the eighteenth century, for example.

Mass-production furniture. We must not forget the productions of the Faubourg Saint-Antoine.[1] The fact is that mass-production furniture has been turned out for centuries, and how many houses are there which are not furnished in this way ! All I ask is that the mass-production furniture of to-day should belong to our own time and that the ridiculous and unsuitable imitations of ancient work should be given up.

Conveyed at the same hours by the same trains to the same sky-scrapers. You are not going to make me believe that up to the fatal moment when my book was published trains started at any old hour, arrived when they liked, and once arrived were broken up and burnt, so that *other* trains could be employed the next day ! Perhaps in those wonderful fairy-tale days the train went to *another* station the next day, in order to preserve a sense of the unexpected !

Identically similar offices. And are they so dissimilar, one from the other, at the present time ? Nearly all are merely converted domestic dwellings, and on the domestic plan, and nearly all exactly the same ; and they make extremely bad offices at that.

Recreations all based on the same model. Is this really so ? All I propose is that right at one's door (and my scheme makes this possible) there should be playing fields for football, tennis and any other games you like. I merely find room for these, and there is certainly no room for them to-day.

Each with his little piece of ground. It seems to me that this has been the dream of every would-be town planner for the last thirty years. Is it seriously suggested that I am wrong in making this possible ?

[1] Or Tottenham Court Road.—F. E.

The individual watering-can is forbidden. Yes, because I have been able, in a purely architectural way, to introduce an automatic system of watering the garden plots ! Are we to treat the watering-can as an important entity, so that we may say, " my own roof-tree . . . my own watering-can ? "

All this dreadful speed, this organization, this terrible uniformity. What we have to do is to replace the *present* terrible uni-

— Je veux qu'en France chaque habitant ait son auto.
— Ce sera le moyen d'empêcher que chaque auto n'en
arrive à avoir sa tête d'habitant.   (Dessin de L. KERN.)

Le Journal, October 2, 1923.

formity by a constantly renewed variety, and this is the aim of my work. Take any street you like in any great town and you will find uniformity everywhere. In my book I try to find a way out.

So much logic taken to its extreme limits, so much " science," so much of the " mechanical," everywhere present, and challenging one on every page. Are these the unpardonable crimes of some architect who has strayed from the fold ? So we reach the point that an architect has no business to be logical ; he ought to be ignorant, and in this twentieth century he ought to avoid

everything that smacks of the " mechanical " ! This is a significant statement appearing in such an important architectural
organ.

Claiming its insolent triumph. So these principles *do*
triumph ! Thank you very much, for this is just what I am
aiming at.

To make one long for "disorder." So now we reach the
stage where Architecture is to lead to disorder !

I have given an analysis of this extract because one finds in
it a perfect example of the catchwords (and how " standardized " they are !) used by those who cling to an old dead past,
and of the methods by which it is sought to blind public
opinion to the growing manifestations of a new spirit in these
matters.

What gives our dreams their daring is that they can be realized.

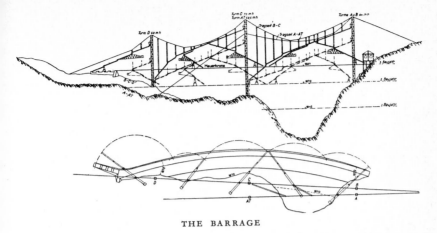

THE BARRAGE

Plan and elevation of the concrete distributors; the whole temporary structure in connection with these has a length of 400 yards and reaches a height of 400 feet. The steel "pylons" can be seen, by means of which the concrete is raised to the necessary level, and the "toboggan-runs" by which it is distributed; these are suspended by a system of cables.

X

OUR TECHNICAL EQUIPMENT

" The annals of humanity contain no duel of nations so gigantic as the Franco-Prussian War; no period of history so fruitful in impressive and grandiose events compressed into a space of a few months."
(From an Introduction to a popular history of the war of 1870–71.)
. . . So they thought in 1871 !

IN order that our enthusiasm may not be tainted with cowardice and that possible support may be emboldened, it is essential, if we are to make a strong assault on compromise and democratic stagnation, to describe clearly the equipment which our forerunners have bequeathed us.

We must show how, when faced with the collective phenomenon which the great city presents to us, neither our initiative, nor our powers, nor the means at our disposal are any longer individual as they once were (and were therefore limited and inefficient), but that they proceed from the intense fusion of every sort of energy, a fusion which is the result of the particular form of progress which has made our own age ; and that these initiatives, these powers and these means form a sort of colossal pyramid whose successive stages are composed of individuals grouped and gathered together, as it were, into a mighty regiment marching under the universal impulse of a common idea. We must also touch on the most recent factor of all, that solidarity between human beings, which is international and indeed intercontinental. To-day, in the twentieth century, a solidarity of thought prevails in every quarter of the globe. No longer can a piece of work result solely from the effort of an individual. A piece of work, an action or an undertaking involves the use of universal methods ; and these result from innumerable contributions in work from every quarter. Here we have a real collaboration. A man is a small thing and his mind may be mediocre ; but he has the equipment of the whole world at his disposal.

This progress—which is so recent—grows day by day ; the age of science has come into its own (it could not do so before, for mechanism did not exist). What do we know of to-morrow except that we shall see transformations which are to-day undreamed of by us ? and even now we have lost our bearings as a result of the rapid changes of the last twenty years. Our fathers, and still more our grandfathers, led quite another kind of life and in a quite different environment. The actual life of to-day is abnormal, and completely unbalanced ; the hostile environment we find around us is insupportable. Nevertheless we have at our disposal the possibility of a universal collaboration in ways and means, which will without any doubt materialize and enable us, before long, to carry out the ideas which our minds have conceived ; one example among many will make this clear.

*

THE BARRAGE

Let us take the case of an immense barrage in process of construction in the Alps. It is a purely technical problem ; patience and minute precision are needed in order to raise the level of the valley and its slopes. A simple multiplication sum will suffice to discover how much water the artificial lake so created will hold. A little use of the slide rule will resolve a few relatively simple formulae. In short, our barrage has to be built so many feet in length and so many in height. It must be of such and such a thickness at its base, and of a relative thickness at the top, given a calculated thrust. An ordinary trained person could work this out.

But the figures themselves are overwhelming ; the quantity of aggregate needed, measured in cubic yards, is colossal. The barrage is being built at a height of over 8,000 feet, on the snow-line. The valley is situated almost at the end of the world, so distant is it from all stations and roads ; in every direction precipices and walls of rock bar the way. Every winter the snow lies sixty feet thick over the confined site of the barrage, and the limit of time available is a short five months in the summer season ; the storms are of a kind usual at such altitudes.

There is not a soul in the vicinity, not a cabin except for the Alpine hut which in summer shelters the mountain climbers. There are no supplies available, no fuel.

Such are the conditions under which the miracle is about to take place.

. . . A Pharaoh would have employed 3,000 men to drag a monolith from its quarry to the temple ; 2,000 boatmen would have toiled three years to transport a granite shrine hewn out of the living rock. One can picture the shouts, the crack of whips, the anguish and martyrdom of these human herds, the indescribable confusion, so barbarous and intolerable !

.   .   .   .

The entrance to the high valley is by a steep pass. You hear a soft musical burden. It is the hum of well-oiled pulleys running along a steel cable. Here is the whole secret : an

overhead system consisting of a double steel cable which is
suspended from steel " pylons " and runs for miles at a height
of some thirty feet above the rocks and grasses. Working hours
are from 5 a.m. to 5 p.m. The whole valley resounds with the
hum. At the far end is the foot of a glacier, and there an
automatic shovel drags through the soil and tears out the
pebbles which will go to form the aggregate after they have
been passed through the crushing machines and along the
endless bands to the washers, the screens, to the automatic
loaders which send along the cable, suspended between the sky
and the earth, an enormous tonnage of ballast which is now
reduced to a uniform size and made fit for its purpose. One
after another, every fifty yards, the containers come up into the
building where the concrete mixers are at work—300 feet above
the dam itself—and automatically empty themselves. From the
opposite direction, from the valley below, from which a funicular
railway drops 2,400 feet into another valley as far as the
mountain station, where a fussy but determined little railway
links up through a hundred rugged and precipitous ways with
the great valley a further 6,000 feet below the dam itself, the
containers move, carrying a sack of cement every time two or
three buckets of gravel have passed by.

By careful timing, the cables, one coming from the glacier
and the other from the distant valley, work more exactly than
a man could with his two hands. And every day tons of
materials in their correct proportions have quietly flowed into
the concrete mixers arranged in a line. High up there in the
mountains, therefore, is the aggregate ; and there the various
materials are mixed in their proportions, moistened to exactly
the right degree and the concrete is made ; this is then poured
quickly into the containers, which are carried sharply up to the
tops of the pylons which overhang the barrage. The concrete
is then automatically tipped out and flows down the flexible
" runs." Imagine a network of cables suspended against the
pure blue sky and forming as it were a series of suspension
bridges across the valley ; these " runs," which in reality are a

L

sort of toboggan-run, descend at carefully calculated angles
from the upper air towards the base of the barrage, and there
finally we come to men at work. They take these immense
serpents by the throat and guide the flow of the concrete to its
proper place ; thus hour after hour, during three short summer
seasons, the concrete flows without pause.

The soft hum accompanies one everywhere ; on waking at
5 a.m. in the hut of the Alpine Club the ear catches the kindly
sound which gives a sense of comfort, of security and order.
There are no human beings about except the twenty or so at
the barrage itself. Here and there, near the machines, a few
hands are oiling or polishing under the eye of the mechanics.
And there are a certain number of cleaners. That is not quite
all, for high up, and seen against the sky, is the giddy spectacle
of a workman coming down one of the toboggan-runs, cleaning
as he descends.

Here is another terrifying sight : a group of workmen want
to go from one end of the barrage to the other ; a platform
descends from above and rises again into the sky with the men
standing on it in a bunch ; it then runs along the cable and
comes down at the other end of the barrage. Seen from the
foot of the barrage the pylons show scarlet, with their coating
of red lead, and the cables white ; the mountains dominate the
scene. It may seem absurd, but one's mind goes back to the
Giants building Valhalla. The gods are on earth and touch a
lever in the machine-room ; an organ plays softly over the
wild landscape ; herds of cows and goats browse on the last
few blades of grass, in the silent splendour of these lofty heights.

You say to yourself : Man is mighty ; he assails Heaven
itself. And in this Tower of Babel we hear the sounds of
French, and the work goes forward. It is most moving, most
captivating. The thing is magnificent !

.   .   .   .

And here is the moral of the barrage :
At the foot of the barrage is a sort of cowboy camp—the
huts in which the workers eat and sleep are perfectly built and

equipped, all standardized and comfortable and as clean as a hospital.

There also is a long hut where those who direct the work live. You call at the hut to see the " mighty captains " of this immense undertaking ; you find three very normal gentlemen, just like yourselves ; the notion that they represent a " new state of mind " would make them roar with laughter. If you praise them because of their work, they protest that all they want is to get through their 600 cubic yards a day. You tell them how moved you have been ; it has no effect. If you talk of their splendid achievement, they take you for a fool. Are these our poets ! It is most upsetting.

" A plant such as you have here," one says, " is a superb foretaste of an age that is fast approaching. When towns are built as you are building your dam . . . when the rebuilding of Paris begins on a large scale, what noble architectural works may we not hope for " . . . and so forth. " Paris!" they exclaim, " do you mean that you want to rebuild the centre of Paris ? But that means destroying it all. What about Beauty ? And the Past ? " (Through the windows you can see the steel Valhalla standing up against the sky.) " But your plant," we continue, " reveals the potentialities of a new epoch and opens up dazzling horizons to our eyes. . . ." " Oh, you think so, do you ? You mean the eight-hour day, jazz, the cinema, and girls who go about with everybody ! . . ."

And so one comes quickly down to earth again.

But it is not really so : here is the lesson the building of the dam can teach us :

(a) The use of the slide rule ; for with it we can resolve every equation. The laws of physics are at the base of all human achievement.

(b) A highly scrupulous overseer, who will rise at 5 a.m. and pull the lever in the machine-room which sets the hum in motion ; who will oversee the oiling of every moving part, and issue his orders as and when needed.

(c) Someone to do the drudgery of getting the plant

together ; for the construction of the dam involves a mountain railway with its engines and trucks, a system of overhead cables, pylons, a system for distributing the aggregate, concrete-making machines and a dredger. All this equipment must be got together.

The chief engineer of the works, by a pure coincidence, happened to be a contractor I knew twenty years ago in a little village where he was putting up small houses. But even at that time one noticed how astonishingly exact his estimates were, and how his modest equipment was yet adequate to meet any emergency. He was one of those very rare men who are always on the spot, a careful and strict supervisor on Sundays as well as week-days, and never relaxing. A born controller. It was *because he never relaxed his attention* that twenty years afterwards he had become the chief engineer of the barrage.

And so we may say that though Nature is multiform, prolific and illimitable, yet man can extract simple laws there-from, with which to make simple equations. Human toil to be successful must be carried out under a condition of *order,* and only this will bring a great undertaking to success. We have no need of great men for great undertakings, though great men have been needed here and there to search out Nature's equations.

And here again is the moral of the dam.

Let us examine more closely the immense mechanical power used in its construction and outlined in para. (*c*) above.

It is, as it were, an international rendezvous of every inventor. On the bobbins of the cables you find the word " France " ; on the railway engines " Leipzig " ; on the pylons and the toboggan runs " U.S.A." ; on the electrical machines " Switzer-land " ; and so on. There are minute units hardly larger than a nut which serve to join the ends of two cables ; on the cast-ings the letters " U.S.A." can be read.

Let us think a little and the miracle explains itself. The whole world is in collaboration nowadays. Any sufficiently ingenious invention, be it as small a thing as a screw or a hook,

NEW YORK: A STREET WITH FIVE LEVELS OF RAILROADS AND
STATIONS (6TH AVENUE)

In the lowest " tunnel " is the main line—the " Pennsylvania Railroad."

LONDON: SUPERIMPOSED UNDERGROUND STATIONS

supplants and pushes out everything else of the same kind and finds its way everywhere. Seas, frontiers, language and local custom are powerless against it. Multiply the phenomenon and you will agree that everything in the way of progress, that is to say, of our technical equipment, is a definite addition to what has gone before. Science has given us the machine. The machine gives us unlimited power. And we in our turn can perform miracles by its means.

We have in our hands a technical equipment which is the sum of man's acquired knowledge.

And armed with this equipment, with this thing that has so suddenly come into being and grown gigantic, we can create *great works*.

That is the moral of the barrage.

We must create *great works*. But in this case the gods of the modern Valhalla are so much brute material incapable of permanently affecting us.

It is a question of soul, of something which we have at heart ; something which is no longer international nor multiple, but individual and cannot be added to by others ; something which is *in a man* and the power of which dies with him. It is a question of *Art*.

*

The men who build the barrage are everyday units, like you and me.

But the barrage itself is magnificent.

Because, even though man is petty and narrow-minded, he has within him the possibility of greatness.

The difficulty is no longer an overwhelming one, it can be subdivided indefinitely into stages ; and each stage can be adapted to the individual. It depends on ourselves to tackle it.

Men can be paltry.

But the thing we call Man is great.

The barrage is great.

What gives our dreams their daring is that they can be realized.

*

PARIS. AT WORK ON THE TUBE, 1907

CONSTRUCTING THE METAL CAISSONS TO BE BURIED IN THE
MARSHY GROUND BORDERING THE SEINE

PARIS : THE PLACE VENDÔME

Let us take the case of Louis XIV.

Here was a king, a great town planner in history, in whose day Paris was nothing but an ant-heap, the fatal consequence of lack of order.

Paris was then a network of overcrowded alleys, just as Dumas describes it. It was difficult to indulge in dreams of architectural beauty in such a confusion. Such a dream required

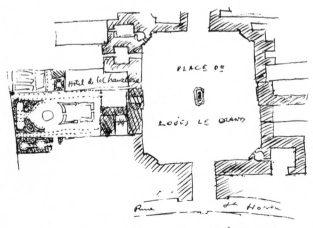

PLAN OF THE PLACE VENDÔME

even a greater temerity than is needed at the present moment, when at least we possess what Louis XIV has left us.

It is useless to say that everything is possible to an absolute monarch ; the same thing might be said of Ministers and their Departments, for they are, potentially at least, absolute monarchs (even if their general slackness prevents their being so in fact).

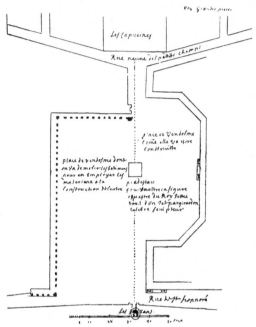

THE PLACE VENDÔME

" *Know by these presents that the portions tinted yellow on this plan within the boundaries of the Hôtel de Vendôme and its dependencies and of the ancient convent of the Capuchins in the Rue Neuve St.-Honoré are for sale. Such as wish to acquire properties abutting on the square will become the sole owners of the arcades His Majesty is now building, and may buy as much frontage as they wish provided it be not less than two arches. Buyers, whether of land abutting on the square or on the neighbouring streets, shall be exempt from payment of tax in respect of the said acquisition, but not from the usual seignorial rights due to the Lords of the Manors in all things according to the Edict of the Council of State dated the 2nd May, 1686, copies of which may be seen at the said Hôtel.*"

No, the important thing was the conception, a conception well thought out and clearly presented.

So Louis XIV issued an edict, to the effect that the Place Vendôme was small and mean ; that the buildings in it were to be demolished and the materials re-used to build a new Place. The plans (given above) showed the rebuilding in accordance with Mansart's designs. The façade to the square was to be built at the King's expense. The ground behind the façades was available for purchase as desired.

Buyers could acquire a portion, larger or smaller, of the façade, regulated by the number of windows. Houses could extend to a considerable depth back from the frontage.

The Place Vendôme is one of the purest jewels in the world's treasury.[1]

*

The vital thing is to have an idea, a conception and a programme.
And the means ?

Do we not possess the means ?

Louis XIV made do with picks and shovels. Even wheelbarrows had only just been invented by Pascal.

And is not big finance, which turns everything into trusts and can even lead us into dreadful wars, now at its height ? The organization of the Place Vendôme by Louis XIV was a tiny affair, and yet the square still stands for our pride and delight.

Here was a king, the last great town planner in history— Louis XIV. Paris was then nothing but an ant-heap, the fatal consequence of lack of order. It was a network of overcrowded alleys. It was difficult to indulge in dreams of architectural

---

[1] There has been a great confusion of ideas here. One of the directors of our urban destinies exclaims : " You call that business of the Place Vendôme clever ? Everybody building as he wanted behind the façade. It is false and immoral, the negation of architecture. Everyone should have his *own façade*. It is a question of fitness."

We are back in the Middle Ages again. The immense breach opened out by Louis XIV and carried still further by Napoleon (*i.e.* in the Rue de Rivoli) is closing up again. . . .

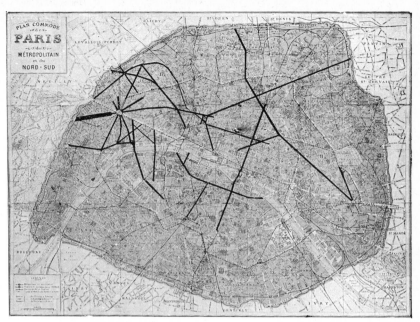

HAUSSMANN'S MAIN SURGICAL OPERATIONS

HAUSSMANN'S EQUIPMENT

153

beauty in such a confusion.   An idea was needed, well thought
out and clearly presented.

Are not our Ministers and their Departments absolute rulers?

In those days the disgrace a man risked might lead him to the
Bastille.   Nowadays, retreat is accompanied by all sorts of little
attentions, solicitude and deference.   It is not even any longer
dangerous to have ideas.

*

The vital thing is to have an idea, a conception, and a programme.
And the means?

Do we not possess the means?

Haussmann cut immense gaps right through Paris, and
carried out the most startling operations.   It seemed as if Paris
would never endure his surgical experiments.

And yet to-day does it not *exist* merely as a consequence of
his daring and courage?

His equipment was meagre ; the shovel, the pick, the wagon,
the trowel, the wheelbarrow, the simple tools of every race
. . . before the mechanical age.

His achievement was truly admirable.   And in destroying
chaos he built up the Emperor's finances !

In those days the French Chambers of Deputies attacked
this dangerous man in stormy scenes.   One day, in an excess of
terror, they accused him of having created a *desert* in the very
centre of Paris !   That desert was the Boulevard Sébastopol
which is now so congested that every expedient is being tried
to relieve it : the policeman's white truncheon, the whistle,
mounted police and electric signals, both visual and aural !
Such is life !

THE GREAT WALL OF CHINA, NEARLY 2,000 MILES IN LENGTH

UNITED STATES: SCHEME FOR A SKY-
SCRAPER CONTAINING TWELVE HOTELS
WITH 6,000 ROOMS: 190 STOREYS

THE PLATFORM OF AN AIRPLANE CARRIER AT SEA

THE PONT DE PÉROLLES (FRIBOURG) 1921

The bridge is built with five spans, each having a width of over 170 feet and a height of over 200 feet.

SECOND PART

LABORATORY WORK, AN INQUIRY INTO THEORY

A definite line of conduct is essential. We need basic principles for modern town planning.

We must create a firm theoretical scheme, and so arrive at the basic principles of modern town planning.

Ancient conditions
still persisting.

Present conditions leading
to the crisis which is only
just beginning.

XI

A CONTEMPORARY CITY

The existing congestion in the centre must be eliminated.

THE use of technical analysis and architectural synthesis
enabled me to draw up my scheme for a contemporary
city of three million inhabitants. The result of my work was
shown in November 1922 at the Salon d'Automne in Paris.
It was greeted with a sort of stupor; the shock of surprise
caused rage in some quarters and enthusiasm in others. The
solution I put forward was a rough one and completely uncompromising. There were no notes to accompany the plans, and,
alas! not everybody can read a plan.[1] I should have had to
be constantly on the spot in order to reply to the fundamental questions which spring from the very depths of human
feelings. Such questions are of profound interest and cannot
remain unanswered. When at a later date it became necessary

[1] As every architect knows to his sorrow.—F. E.

that this book should be written, a book in which I could formulate the new principles of Town Planning, I resolutely decided *first of all* to find answers to these fundamental questions. I have used two kinds of argument : first, those essentially human ones which start from the mind or the heart or the physiology of our sensations as a basis ; secondly, historical and statistical arguments. Thus I could keep in touch with what is fundamental and at the same time be master of the environment in which all this takes place.

In this way I hope I shall have been able to help my reader to take a number of steps by means of which he can reach a sure and certain position. So that when I unroll my plans I can have the happy assurance that his astonishment will no longer be stupefaction nor his fears mere panic.

*

A CONTEMPORARY CITY OF THREE MILLION INHABITANTS

Proceeding in the manner of the investigator in his laboratory, I have avoided all special cases, and all that may be accidental, and I have assumed an ideal site to begin with. My object was not to overcome the existing state of things, but *by constructing a theoretically water-tight formula to arrive at the fundamental principles of modern town planning*. Such fundamental principles, if they are genuine, can serve as the skeleton of any system of modern town planning ; being as it were the *rules* according to which development will take place. We shall then be in a position to take a special case, no matter what : whether it be Paris, London, Berlin, New York or some small town. Then, as a result of what we have learnt, we can take control and decide in what direction the forthcoming battle is to be waged. For the desire to rebuild any great city in a modern way is to engage in a formidable battle. Can you imagine people engaging in a battle without knowing their objectives ? Yet that is exactly what is happening. The authorities are compelled to do something, so they give the police white sleeves or set them on horseback, they invent sound signals and light signals, they propose to put bridges over streets or moving pavements under the streets ; more garden cities are suggested, or it is decided to suppress the tramways, and so on. And these decisions are reached in a sort of frantic haste in order, as it were, to hold a wild beast at bay. That BEAST is the great city. It is infinitely more powerful than all these devices. And it is just beginning to wake. What will to-morrow bring forth to cope with it ?

We must have some rule of conduct.[1]

We must have fundamental principles for modern town planning.

SITE.

A level site is the ideal site. In all those places where traffic becomes over-intensified the level site gives a chance of a normal solution to the problem. Where there is less traffic, differences in level matter less.

The river flows far away from the city. The river is a kind of liquid railway, a goods station and a sorting house. In a decent house the servants' stairs do not go through the drawing-room—even if the maid is charming (or if the little boats delight the loiterer leaning on a bridge).

POPULATION.

This consists of the citizens proper ; of suburban dwellers ; and of those of a mixed kind.

[1] New suggestions shower on us. Their inventors and those who believe in them have their little thrill. It is so easy for them to believe in them. But what if they are based on grave errors ? How are we to distinguish between what is reasonable and an over-poetical dream ? The leading newspapers accept everything with enthusiasm. One of them said, " The cities of to-morrow must be built on new virgin soil." But no, this is not true ! We must go to the old cities, all our inquiries confirm it. One of our leading papers supports the suggestion made by one of our greatest and most reasonable architects, who for once gives us bad counsel in proposing to erect round about Paris a ring of sky-scrapers. The idea is romantic enough, but it cannot be defended. The sky-scrapers must be built *in the centre* and not on the periphery.

(*a*) Citizens are of the city : those who work and live in it.

(*b*) Suburban dwellers are those who work in the outer industrial zone and who do not come into the city : they live in garden cities.

(*c*) The mixed sort are those who work in the business parts of the city but bring up their families in garden cities.

To classify these divisions (and so make possible the transmutation of these recognized types) is to attack the most important problem in town planning, for such a classification would define the areas to be allotted to these three sections and the delimitation of their boundaries.   This would enable us to formulate and resolve the following problems :

1. The *City*, as a business and residential centre.

2. The *Industrial City* in relation to the *Garden Cities* (*i.e.* the question of transport).

3. The *Garden Cities* and the *daily transport* of the workers.

Our first requirement will be an organ that is compact, rapid, lively and concentrated : this is the City with its well-organized centre.   Our second requirement will be another organ, supple, extensive and elastic ; this is *the Garden City* on the periphery.

Lying between these two organs, we must *require the legal establishment* of that absolute necessity, a protective zone which allows of extension, *a reserved zone* of woods and fields, a fresh-air reserve.

DENSITY OF POPULATION.

The more dense the population of a city is the less are the distances that have to be covered.   The moral, therefore, is that we must *increase the density of the centres of our cities, where business affairs are carried on.*

LUNGS.

Work in our modern world becomes more intensified day by day, and its demands affect our nervous system in a way that grows more and more dangerous. Modern toil demands quiet and fresh air, not stale air.

The towns of to-day can only increase in density at the expense of the open spaces which are the lungs of a city.

We must *increase the open spaces and diminish the distances to be covered*. Therefore the centre of the city must be constructed *vertically*.

The city's residential quarters must no longer be built along " corridor-streets," full of noise and dust and deprived of light.

It is a simple matter to build urban dwellings away from the streets, without small internal courtyards and with the windows looking on to large parks ; and this whether our housing schemes are of the type with " set-backs " or built on the " cellular " principle.

THE STREET.

The street of to-day is still the old bare ground which has been paved over, and under which a few tube railways have been run.

The modern street in the true sense of the word is a new type of organism, a sort of stretched-out workshop, a home for many complicated and delicate organs, such as gas, water and electric mains. It is contrary to all economy, to all security, and to all sense to bury these important service mains. They ought to be accessible throughout their length. The various storeys of this stretched-out workshop will each have their own particular functions. If this type of street, which I have called a " workshop," is to be realized, it becomes as much a matter of *construction* as are the houses with which it is customary to flank it, and the bridges which carry it over valleys and across rivers.

The modern street should be a masterpiece of civil engineering and no longer a job for navvies.

The " corridor-street " should be tolerated no longer, for it poisons the houses that border it and leads to the construction of small internal courts or " wells."

TRAFFIC.

Traffic can be classified more easily than other things.

To-day traffic is not classified—it is like dynamite flung at hazard into the street, killing pedestrians. Even so, *traffic does not fulfill its function*. This sacrifice of the pedestrian leads nowhere. If we classify traffic we get :

(*a*) Heavy goods traffic.

(*b*) Lighter goods traffic, *i.e.* vans, etc., which make short journeys in all directions.

(*c*) Fast traffic, which covers a large section of the town.

Three kinds of roads are needed, and in superimposed storeys :

(*a*) Below-ground [1] there would be the street for heavy traffic. This storey of the houses would consist merely of concrete piles, and between them large open spaces which would form a sort of clearing-house where heavy goods traffic could load and unload.

(*b*) At the ground floor level of the buildings there would be the complicated and delicate network of the ordinary streets taking traffic in every desired direction.

(*c*) Running north and south, and east and west, and forming the two great axes of the city, there would be great *arterial roads for fast one-way traffic* built on immense reinforced concrete bridges 120 to 180 yards in width and approached every half-mile or so by subsidiary roads from ground level. These arterial roads could therefore be joined at any given point, so that even at the highest speeds the town can be traversed and the suburbs reached without having to negotiate any cross-roads

The number of existing streets *should be diminished by two-thirds*. The number of crossings depends directly on the

---

[1] I say " below-ground," but it would be more exact to say at what we call *basement level*, for if my town, built on concrete piles, were realized (see *Towards a New Architecture*, Chap. IV), this " basement " would no longer be buried under the earth. See also Chapter XII of this volume : " Housing Schemes on the ' Cellular ' Principle."

number of streets ; and *cross-roads are an enemy to traffic.*
The number of existing streets was fixed at a remote epoch
in history. The perpetuation of the boundaries of properties
has, almost without exception, preserved even the faintest
tracks and footpaths of the old village and made streets of them,
and sometimes even an avenue (see Chapter I : " The Pack-
Donkey's Way and Man's Way ").

The result is that we have cross-roads every fifty yards,
even every twenty yards or ten yards. And this leads to the
ridiculous traffic congestion we all know so well.

The distance between two 'bus stops or two tube stations
gives us the necessary unit for the distance between streets,
though this unit is conditional on the speed of vehicles and the
walking capacity of pedestrians. So an average measure of
about 400 yards would give the normal separation between
streets, and make a standard for urban distances. My city is
conceived on the gridiron system with streets every 400 yards,
though occasionally these distances are subdivided to give
streets every 200 yards.

This triple system of superimposed levels answers every
need of motor traffic (lorries, private cars, taxis, 'buses) because
it provides for rapid and *mobile* transit.

Traffic running on fixed rails is only justified if it is in the
form of a convoy carrying an immense load ; it then becomes
a sort of extension of the underground system or of trains dealing with suburban traffic. *The tramway has no right to exist in
the heart of the modern city.*

If the city thus consists of plots about 400 yards square,
this will give us sections of about 40 acres in area, and the
density of population will vary from 50,000 down to 6,000,
according as the " lots " are developed for business or for
residential purposes. The natural thing, therefore, would be
to continue to apply our unit of distance as it exists in the Paris
tubes to-day (namely, 400 yards) and to put a station in the
middle of each plot.

Following the two great axes of the city, two " storeys "

below the arterial roads for fast traffic, would run the tubes
leading to the four furthest points of the garden city suburbs,
and linking up with the metropolitan network (see the next
chapter). At a still lower level, and again following these two
main axes, would run the one-way loop systems for suburban
traffic, and below these again the four great main lines serving
the provinces and running north, south, east and west. These
main lines would end at the Central Station, or better still
might be connected up by a loop system.

THE STATION.

There is only one station. The only place for the station is
in the centre of the city. It is the natural place for it, and there
is no reason for putting it anywhere else. The railway station
is the hub of the wheel.

The station would be an essentially subterranean building.
Its roof, which would be two storeys above the natural ground
level of the city, would form the aerodrome for aero-taxis.
This aerodrome (linked up with the main aerodrome in the
protected zone) must be in close contact with the tubes, the
suburban lines, the main lines, the main arteries and the administrative services connected with all these. (See the plan of the
Station in the following chapter.)

THE PLAN OF THE CITY

The basic principles we must follow are these :

1. We must de-congest the centres of our cities.
2. We must augment their density.
3. We must increase the means for getting about.
4. We must increase parks and open spaces.

At the very centre we have the STATION with its landing
stage for aero-taxis.

Running north and south, and east and west, we have the

MAIN ARTERIES for fast traffic, forming elevated roadways 120 feet wide.

At the base of the sky-scrapers and all round them we have a great open space 2,400 yards by 1,500 yards, giving an area of 3,600,000 square yards, and occupied by gardens, parks and avenues. In these parks, at the foot of and round the sky-scrapers, would be the restaurants and cafés, the luxury shops, housed in buildings with receding terraces : here too would be the theatres, halls and so on ; and here the parking places or garage shelters.

The sky-scrapers are designed purely for business purposes.

On the left we have the great public buildings, the museums, the municipal and administrative offices. Still further on the left we have the " Park " (which is available for further logical development of the heart of the city).

On the right, and traversed by one of the arms of the main arterial roads, we have the warehouses, and the industrial quarters with their goods stations.

All round the city is the *protected zone* of woods and green fields.

Further beyond are the *garden cities*, forming a wide encircling band.

Then, right in the midst of all these, we have the *Central Station*, made up of the following elements :

(*a*) The landing-platform ; forming an aerodrome of 200,000 square yards in area.

(*b*) The entresol or mezzanine ; at this level are the raised tracks for fast motor traffic : the only crossing being gyratory.

(*c*) The ground floor where are the entrance halls and booking offices for the tubes, suburban, main line and air traffic.

(*d*) The " basement " : here are the tubes which serve the city and the main arteries.

(*e*) The " sub-basement " : here are the suburban lines running on a one-way loop.

(*f*) The " sub-sub-basement " : here are the main lines (going north, south, east and west).

THE CITY.

Here we have twenty-four sky-scrapers capable each of housing 10,000 to 50,000 employees ; this is the business and hotel section, etc., and accounts for 400,000 to 600,000 inhabitants.

The residential blocks, of the two main types already mentioned, account for a further 600,000 inhabitants.

The garden cities give us a further 2,000,000 inhabitants, or more.

In the great central open space are the cafés, restaurants, luxury shops, halls of various kinds, a magnificent forum descending by stages down to the immense parks surrounding it, the whole arrangement providing a spectacle of order and vitality.

DENSITY OF POPULATION.

(*a*) The sky-scraper : 1,200 inhabitants to the acre.

(*b*) The residential blocks with set-backs : 120 inhabitants to the acre. These are the luxury dwellings.

(*c*) The residential blocks on the " cellular " system, with a similar number of inhabitants.

This great density gives us our necessary shortening of distances and ensures rapid intercommunication.

Note.—The average density to the acre of Paris in the heart of the town is 146, and of London 63 ; and of the over-crowded quarters of Paris 213, and of London 169.

OPEN SPACES.

Of the area (*a*), 95 per cent of the ground is open (squares, restaurants, theatres).

Of the area (*b*), 85 per cent. of the ground is open (gardens, sports grounds).

Of the area (*c*), 48 per cent. of the ground is open (gardens, sports grounds).

TWO VIEWS, TO THE SAME SCALE
AND SEEN FROM THE SAME
ANGLE: ONE OF MANHATTAN AND
THE OTHER THE CENTRE OF "A
CONTEMPORARY CITY"

The contrast is startling.

EDUCATIONAL AND CIVIC CENTRES, UNIVERSITIES, MUSEUMS OF ART AND INDUSTRY, PUBLIC SERVICES, COUNTY HALL.

The " Jardin anglais." (The city can extend here, if necessary.)

Sports grounds : Motor racing track, Racecourse, Stadium, Swimming baths, etc.

THE PROTECTED ZONE (which will be the property of the city), with its AERODROME.

A zone in which all building would be prohibited ; reserved for the growth of the city as laid down by the municipality : it would consist of woods, fields, and sports grounds. The forming of a " protected zone " by continual purchase of small properties in the immediate vicinity of the city is one of the most essential and urgent tasks which a municipality can pursue. It would eventually represent a tenfold return on the capital invested.

INDUSTRIAL QUARTERS.[1]

TYPES OF BUILDINGS EMPLOYED.

For business : sky-scrapers sixty storeys high with no internal wells or courtyards (see the following chapter).

Residential buildings with " set-backs," of six double storeys ; again with no internal wells : the flats looking on either side on to immense parks.

Residential buildings on the " cellular " principle, with

---

[1] In this section I make new suggestions in regard to the industrial quarters : they have been content to exist too long in disorder, dirt and in a hand-to-mouth way. And this is absurd, for Industry, when it is on a properly ordered basis, should develop in an orderly fashion. A portion of the industrial district could be constructed of ready-made sections by using standard units for the various kinds of buildings needed. Fifty per cent. of the site would be reserved for this purpose. In the event of considerable growth, provision would thus be made for moving them into a different district where there was more space. Bring about " *standardization* " in the building of a works and you would have mobility instead of the crowding which results when factories become impossibly congested.

" hanging gardens," looking on to immense parks ; again no internal wells. These are " service-flats " of the most modern kind.

GARDEN CITIES

Their Æsthetic, Economy, Perfection and Modern Outlook.

A simple phrase suffices to express the necessities of to-morrow : WE MUST BUILD IN THE OPEN. The lay-out must be of a purely geometrical kind, with all its many and delicate implications.

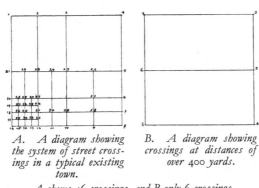

A.   A diagram showing the system of street cross-ings in a typical existing town.

B.   A diagram showing crossings at distances of over 400 yards.

A shows 46 crossings, and B only 6 crossings.

The city of to-day is a dying thing because it is not geome-trical. To build in the open would be to replace our present haphazard arrangements, *which are all we have to-day*, by a *uniform* lay-out. Unless we do this *there is no salvation*.

The result of a true geometrical lay-out is *repetition*.

The result of repetition is a *standard*, the perfect form (*i.e.* the creation of standard types). A geometrical lay-out means that mathematics play their part. There is no first-rate human production but has geometry at its base. It is of the very essence of Architecture. To introduce uniformity into the building of the city we must *industrialize building*. Building is the one economic activity which has so far resisted industrialization.

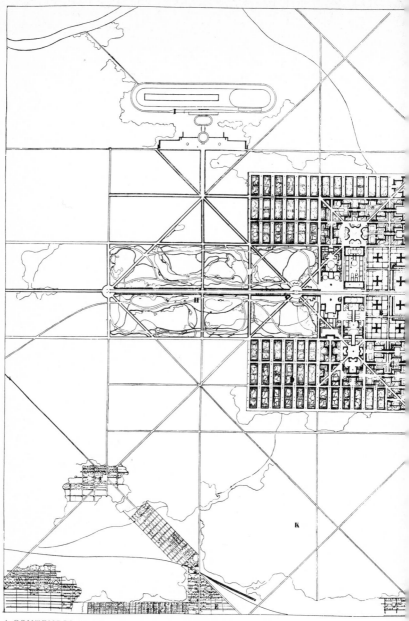

A CONTEMPORARY CITY

The heavy black lines represent the areas built upon. Everything else is either streets or open spaces. Strictly speaking the city is an immense park. Its lay-out furnishes a multitude of architectural aspects of infinitely varying forms. If the reader, for instance, follows out a given route on this map he will be astonished by the variety he encounters. Yet distances are shorter than in the cities of to-day, for there is a greater density of population.

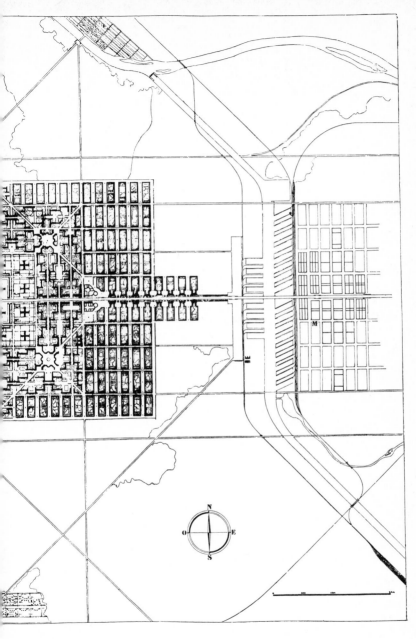

A. Station.
B. Sky-scraper.
C. Housing blocks with " set-backs."
D. Housing blocks on the " cellular " system.
E. Garden cities.

G. Public Services.
H. Park.
I. Sports.
K. Protected zone.
M. Warehouses, Industrial city, Goods station.

A CONTEMPORARY CITY

Panoramic view of the city. In the foreground are the woods and fields of the protected zone. The Great Central Station can be seen in the centre and the two main tracks for fast motor tr crossing one another.

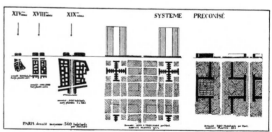

A diagram showing the increase in size of building sites from the fourteenth to the eighteenth and nineteenth centuries. In the nineteenth century the Boulevard Haussmann again offered the " corridor-street " as a solution. But in this plan I allow for sky-scrapers at intervals of 400 yards and for blocks of dwellings with " set-backs." The magnification of the site unit is in proportion to the evolution that has taken place and to the means at our disposal.

along the hills on the horizon and beyond the foliage of the protected zone can just be seen the
Garden Cities.

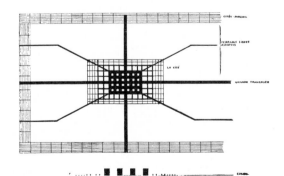

SYSTÈME PRÉCONISÉ
RÉSEAU DES RUES

*A diagram showing the relative importance of streets in a great city. The black
lines give the width of the streets. This system, which indicates what is needed
under the new conditions, is absolutely contrary to the present state of things (see the
diagram at the beginning of this chapter).*

It has thus escaped the march of progress, with the result that the cost of building is still abnormally high.

The architect, from a professional point of view, has become a twisted sort of creature. He has grown to love irregular sites, claiming that they inspire him with original ideas for getting round them. Of course he is wrong. For nowadays the only building that can be undertaken must be either for the rich or built at a loss (as, for instance, in the case of municipal housing schemes), or else by jerry-building and so robbing the inhabitant of all amenities. A motor-car which is achieved by mass production is a masterpiece of comfort, precision, balance and good taste. A house built to order (on an " interesting " site) is a masterpiece of incongruity—a monstrous thing.

If the builder's yard were reorganized on the lines of standardization and mass production we might have gangs of workmen as keen and intelligent as mechanics.

The mechanic dates back only twenty years, yet already he forms the highest caste of the working world.

The mason dates . . . from time immemorial ! He bangs away with feet and hammer. He smashes up everything round him, and the plant entrusted to him falls to pieces in a few months. The spirit of the mason must be disciplined by making him part of the severe and exact machinery of the industrialized builder's yard.

The cost of building would fall in the proportion of 10 to 2.

The wages of the labourers would fall into definite categories; to each according to his merits and service rendered.

The " interesting " or erratic site absorbs every creative faculty of the architect and wears him out. What results is equally erratic : lopsided abortions ; a specialist's solution which can only please other specialists.

We must build *in the open :* both within the city and around it.

Then having worked through every necessary technical stage and using absolute ECONOMY, we shall be in a position to experience the intense joys of a creative art which is based on geometry.

THE CITY AND ITS ÆSTHETIC

(The plan of a city which is here presented is a direct consequence of purely geometric considerations.)

A new unit *on a large scale* (400 yards) inspires everything. Though the gridiron arrangement of the streets every 400 yards (sometimes only 200) is uniform (with a consequent ease in finding one's way about), no two streets are in any way alike. This is where, in a magnificent contrapuntal symphony, the forces of geometry come into play.

Suppose we are entering the city by way of the Great Park. Our fast car takes the special elevated motor track between the majestic sky-scrapers : as we approach nearer there is seen the repetition against the sky of the twenty-four sky-scrapers ; to our left and right on the outskirts of each particular area are the municipal and administrative buildings ; and enclosing the space are the museums and university buildings.

Then suddenly we find ourselves at the feet of the first skyscrapers. But here we have, not the meagre shaft of sunlight which so faintly illumines the dismal streets of New York, but an immensity of space. The whole city is a Park. The terraces stretch out over lawns and into groves. Low buildings of a horizontal kind lead the eye on to the foliage of the trees. Where are now the trivial *Procuracies?* Here is the CITY with its crowds living in peace and pure air, where noise is smothered under the foliage of green trees. The chaos of New York is overcome. Here, bathed in light, stands the modern city.

Our car has left the elevated track and has dropped its speed of sixty miles an hour to run gently through the residential quarters. The " set-backs " [1] permit of vast architectural perspectives. There are gardens, games and sports grounds. And sky everywhere, as far as the eye can see. The square silhouettes of the terraced roofs stand clear against the sky, bordered with the verdure of the hanging gardens. The

[1] As before, this refers to set-backs *on plan ;* buildings " à redents," *i.e.* with projecting salients.—F. E.

uniformity of the units that compose the picture throw into relief the firm lines on which the far-flung masses are constructed. Their outlines softened by distance, the sky-scrapers raise immense geometrical façades all of glass, and in them is reflected the blue glory of the sky. An overwhelming sensation. Immense but radiant prisms.

And in every direction we have a varying spectacle : our " gridiron " is based on a unit of 400 yards, but it is strangely modified by architectural devices ! (The " set-backs " are in counterpoint, on a unit of 600 × 400.)

The traveller in his airplane, arriving from Constantinople or Pekin it may be, suddenly sees appearing through the wavering lines of rivers and patches of forests that clear imprint which marks a city which has grown in accordance with the spirit of man : the mark of the human brain at work.

As twilight falls the glass sky-scrapers seem to flame.

This is no dangerous futurism, a sort of literary dynamite flung violently at the spectator. It is a spectacle organized by an Architecture which uses plastic resources for the modulation of forms seen in light.

A city made for speed is made for success.

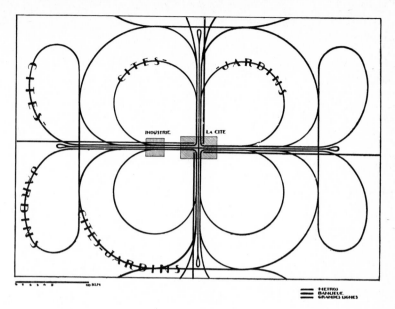

RAILWAY SYSTEM: SUBURBAN AND MAIN LINES

The inter-urban system; the tubes, following the main arteries; the outer loop system of one-way traffic; the main lines.

XII

THE WORKING DAY

THE following considerations are not fanciful, they are merely, once again, the consequences of a continuous train of thought taken to its logical conclusions, and omitting special cases. Pure reason leads us in the end to a fixed rule by which we can solve special cases

*

It is 9 a.m.

From its four vomitories, each 250 yards wide, the station disgorges the travellers from the suburbs. The trains, running in one direction only, follow one another at one-minute intervals. (In Berlin at the " Zoo " station, where many lines meet, this masterpiece of precision has been in operation for years.) The station square is so enormous that everybody can make straight to his work without crowding or difficulty.

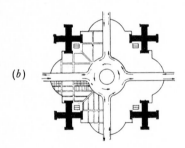

(a)

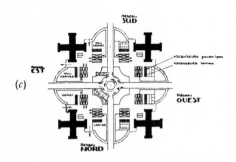

(b)

(c)

Underground, the tube taps the suburban lines at various points and discharges its passengers into the basements of the sky-scrapers, which gradually fill up. Every sky-scraper is a tube station.

A sky-scraper is, in fact, a whole district, but verticalized! 10,000 to 50,000 employees pass their day in it, each with a minimum superficial area of ten square yards to work in. The original and primitive conception of the sky-scraper comes to us from America; but if the disposition of these

THE GREAT CENTRAL STATION

(a) *Upper level. The landing-stage for taxi-planes ; 250,000 sq. yards.*
(b) *Mezzanine level. The crossing for fast motor traffic.*
(c) *Ground level. Showing the access to the various railway lines ; the booking-halls, etc.*

shown in my scheme is compared with the photograph on
p. 169 of New York, where the sky-scraper completely
holds up Manhattan, it will be seen how great is the contrast
between the latter and a rational and clear conception where a
large outlook has been the
deciding factor in the relation to each other of these
indispensable elements. In
New York 20,000 people
invade a narrow street at
practically one moment, and
the result is complete chaos;
all fast traffic is paralyzed
and the idea for which the
sky-scraper stands is robbed
of all significance. Created
for the purpose of de-
congestion, actually it slows
up all traffic and is, in fact,
a powerful factor for congestion. The result is that
people cry out against the
sky-scraper and the vertically
built city; and because of
the need to get about quickly, against the type of city
which is spread out over a
large area. So we have a

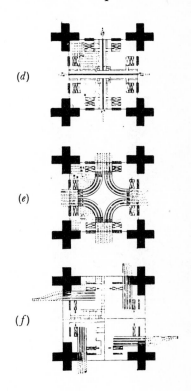

(d) *First level below ground : The Tubes (the main crossing).*
(e) *Second level below ground : Local and suburban lines.*
(f) *Third level below ground : The Main lines. (Cf. in a later chapter the
" Voisin " plan for Paris, where the main line system is designed for
continuous or " through " traffic by means of loops.*

*The entrance halls in connection with each system are exactly opposite the
exits, in order to avoid crowding or confusion, i.e. everything is on the " one-
way " system.*
*Given the immense spaces at our disposal, the technical staff for each system
can be housed on the spot. The four sky-scrapers abutting on the Central
Station house the offices of the various lines.*

new paradox. Since New York (Manhattan) is to some extent
an absurdity, the whole idea is vehemently attacked. The
truth is that the sky-scraper, as we have it in New York, will
not do, for by means of it New York has increased its density
to too great an extent, without proper provision for the
necessary approaches. New York is wrong, but the sky-
scraper remains a noble instrument. But if you are going to

NEW YORK : CONGESTION

increase the density of your population, you must at the same
time make full provision for getting it away. There are two
sides of a medal ; one cannot exist without the other.

In a few moments the city fills up. Work begins, and
speeded up by efficient organization, goes on busily in luminous
and even radiant offices whose immense windows open full on
the sky and the lofty horizon, where the air is pure and noise
far distant. A friend once said to me, " No intelligent man

NEW YORK : CONGESTION

THE 6,000 EMPLOYEES OF AN AMERICAN WORKS
In the background the works themselves

ever looks out of his window ; his window is made of ground
glass ; its only function is to let in light, not to look out of."
Such a feeling is only too appropriate in a congested city where
the disorder is painful to witness ; it might perhaps even be
appropriate in a paradoxical sort of way, in the case of a very
sublime, a too sublime view. Yet, if I climb up to the platforms of the Eiffel Tower, the very act of mounting gives me a

VIEW FROM THE EIFFEL TOWER

feeling of gladness ; the moment is a joyful one, and also a
solemn one. And in proportion as the horizon widens more and
more, one's thought seems to take on a larger and more comprehensive cast : similarly, if everything in the physical sphere
widens out, if the lungs expand more fully and the eye takes in
vast distances, so too the spirit is roused to a vital activity.
Optimism fills the mind. For a wide horizontal perspective
can deeply influence us at the expense of little actual trouble.
Remember that up till now our horizons have never been more

than those revealed to eyes quite close to the earth's surface ;
Alpine climbers alone enjoyed the intoxication of great heights.

From the Eiffel Tower and its platforms at heights of 300,
600 and 900 feet, our horizontal vision is dealing with vast
subjects which move and influence us deeply.

Such offices will give us the feeling of " look-outs " dominat-
ing an ordered world. And actually these sky-scrapers will

VIEW FROM THE TOP OF THE EIFFEL TOWER

contain the city's brains, the brains of the whole nation. They
stand for all the careful working-out and organization on which
the general activity is based. Everything is concentrated in
them : apparatus for abolishing time and space, telephones,
cables and wireless ; the banks, business affairs and the control
of industry ; finance, commerce, specialization. The station is
in the midst of the sky-scrapers, the Tubes run below them and
the tracks for fast traffic are at their base. And all around are
vast open spaces. There need be no limit to the number of

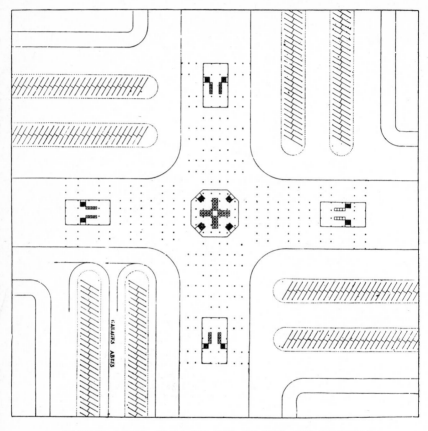

GROUND LEVEL PLAN OF ONE OF THE SKY-SCRAPERS

The space is entirely free save for the numerous steel piles which carry the sixty storeys from base to roof, a total height of nearly 700 feet. Only the lift-halls and stairways are enclosed. In each angle, between the wings of the building, are parking places. All traffic is gyratory.

motor vehicles, for immense covered parking areas linked up by subterranean passages would collect together the host on wheels which camps in the city each day and is the result of rapid *individual* transit. The airplanes too would land in the centre, on the roof of the station, and who knows whether soon it will not be equally possible for them to land on the roofs of the sky-scrapers, from thence without loss of time to link up with the

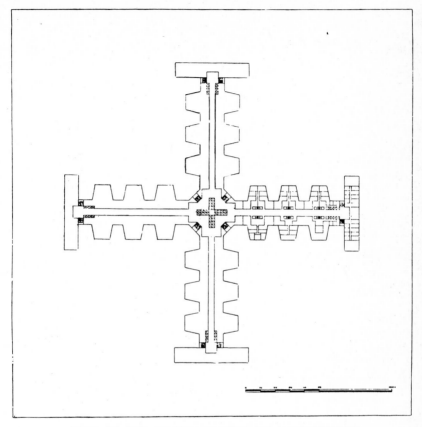

PLAN OF ONE OF THE FLOORS OF A SKY-SCRAPER

*It is in the form of a cross, thus doing away with an internal court and giving
a maximum stability.   The façades are deeply serrated and form veritable
traps for light.   There are five groups of lifts and stairways.   The right
wing suggests one manner of dividing up for offices.   The capacity of a sky-
scraper 460 feet long is 30,000 employees, allowing 10 square yards per
person : that of one 540 feet long would be 40,000.*

provinces and other countries.[1]   From every point of the com-
pass the main railway lines come straight to the centre.

  [1] For the moment, the airport allowed for in the centre is a rank for air-taxis
connecting up with the aerodrome in the protected zone.   Means of landing are
not yet sufficiently perfect to allow the large transcontinental airplane to make its
way safely to the heart of the city.
   Similarly, the problem of landing upon the roofs or terraces of dwellings remains
equally unresolved.   " Domestic " aviation still seems to be some way off.

This is the ideal city. A model city for commerce ! Is it the mere fancy of some neurotic passion for speed ? But, surely, speed lies on this side of mere dreams ; it is a brutal necessity.[1] One can only come to this conclusion ; that the city

[1] " Indeed, the conquest of speed has always been the dream of mankind, yet it has only taken shape in the last hundred years. Before then the stages in the conquest of speed were incredibly distant one from the other. For an immense period of time, man could only move at the rate at which his own limbs would take him, and all his progress, apart from sails, consisted in using the speed of animals.

" Mankind is, in fact, one of the slowest animals in creation. A sort of caterpillar dragging himself with difficulty on the surface of the terrestrial crust. The most part of creation moves quicker than this biped so ill-constructed for speed, and if we imagined a race between all the creatures of the globe, man would certainly be among the ' also rans ' and would probably tie with the sheep." (From the " Reign of Speed " by Philippe Girardet, in the *Mercure de France*, 1923.)

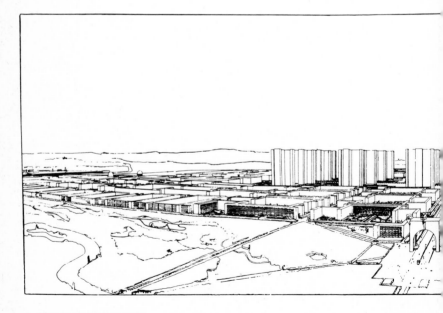

A CONTEMPORARY CITY
A panoramic view of the city and its protected zones of woods and fields.

which can achieve speed will achieve success—and this is an obvious truth. What is the good of regretting the Golden Age ! Work to-day is more intense, and is carried on at a quicker rate. Actually the whole question becomes one of daily intercommunication with a view to settling the state of the market and the conditions of labour. The more rapid this intercommunication can be made, the more will business be expedited. It is likely, therefore, that the working day in the sky-scraper will be a shorter one, thanks to the sky-scraper.

Then, perhaps, the working day may finish soon after midday. The city will empty as though by a deep breath. The garden cities will play their full part. And, on the other hand, in the

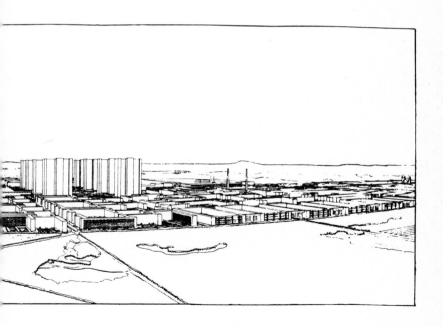

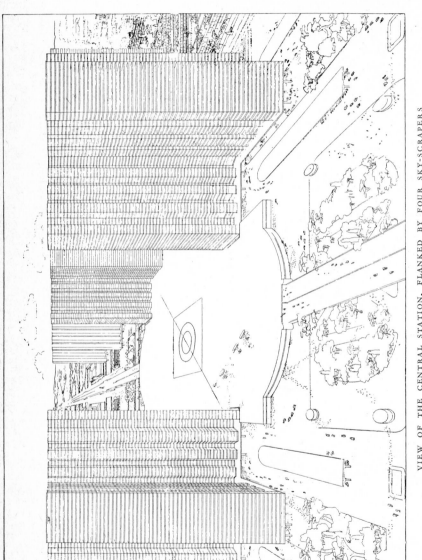

VIEW OF THE CENTRAL STATION, FLANKED BY FOUR SKY-SCRAPERS

The tracks for fast motor traffic pass under the aerodrome. The unobstructed and open ground-floor levels of the sky-scrapers can be seen, as can the piles or "stilts" on which they are built. Covered car-parking places can be perceived on either side. To the right are restaurants, shops, etc., set amidst trees and open spaces.

city itself the residential quarters will offer new living conditions to these new men of a mechanical age.

(We must not forget that our grandfathers rode about in landaus.)

Note.—It bores me more than I can say to describe, like some minor prophet, this future City of the Blest. It makes me imagine I have become a Futurist, a sensation I do not at all appreciate. I feel as though I were leaving on one side the crude realities of existence for the pleasures of automatic lucubrations !

On the other hand, how thrilling it is, before one sets pen to paper, to work out on a drawing-board this world which is almost upon us, for then there are no words to ring false and only facts count.

Our concern, then, must be with precise inventions, fundamental conceptions, and organisms that are likely to endure. Everything has to be allowed for at once. Set the problem, arrange it and adjust it, make it hang together, and still keep in mind the indispensable poetry which alone, when all is said and done, can move us to enthusiasm and inspire us to action.

What I have called an automatic lucubration does not lie in this difficult pursuit of a solution on the drawing-board. It is an act of faith in our own age. In the deepest part of myself I believe in it. I believe in it for the future and not merely because of the formulas that gave the equation, and I believe in it amid all the difficulties of special cases. But we can never have too clear or exact a conception in our minds if we are to solve the problems of special cases.

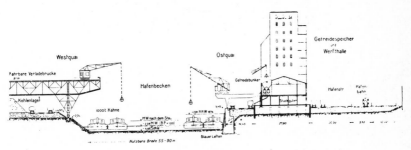

This diagram shows the rational methods by which useful operations are elaborated.

A BUILDING

All that remains is to glaze it !

Already in the month of May, on the Champs Élysées, half the chestnuts lining the avenue have their leaves withered ; the buds have been unable to blossom, and the tiny abortions of leaves are curled tightly up like a shrivelled hand.

. . . .

It is admitted that the third generation to live in our great cities is generally sterile.

The above might well be taken as an image of perfect harmony.

XIII

THE HOURS OF REPOSE

THE eight-hour day.

Some day it may be the six-hour day.

Pessimistic and worried intellectuals have been known to say, "What a prospect! How will so much free time be employed, how can the workers make use of these unoccupied hours?"

The answer is that they must be filled.

It is obvious that here again we have an architectural problem; a problem of housing and town planning; of the organization of residential quarters; of arrangements for using our lungs to the full, for after the day's work is done comes the time when we can breathe freely.

Even now, without waiting for all that might be demanded of architecture and town planning, games and sports have become a real part of our lives. We have found the salutary answer to the harmful forces of the past.

*

I was lucky enough to make the acquaintance of M. Forestier, a Civil Servant in the Department of Woods and Forests,[1] landscape-gardener-architect for the Bois de Boulogne and the planting of trees in Paris. He is a man of very great experience and has made a life study of trees and flowers and the conditions under which they thrive. He knows also what the physical body needs to make it function adequately. He was quite unaware of my work in regard to town planning, yet all he said to me was a confirmation from the practical view-point of my theoretical discoveries.

What he said was this : " In the Department which deals with the growth of Paris the aim is to arrange housing in the suburbs on the lines of the garden city, so that the people may live under health conditions. Well and good ! But day after day the inhabitants of these garden cities have to work in the very centre of the city ; yet that centre remains untouched. In the centre of the city the narrow streets are bottled up between lofty buildings, and the poisonous exhaust gases of the motor traffic cannot get away. This, of course, produces an unhealthy state of affairs not only in the streets but in the houses themselves. These moving masses of infected air affect the surrounding garden cities. Thus any good effects from the proposed remedy are destroyed by the survival of old and bad conditions in the heart of the city.

" Exhaust gases and tar dust have the most appalling effects on our organisms. It has been observed that individuals who, owing to their work, are directly exposed to these emanations, eventually lose the faculty to procreate and become impotent ;

----

[1] *Eaux et Forêts.*—F. E.

and it is generally acknowledged that the third generation to live in a town is sterile.[1]

" The trees suffer terribly. You can see them by the end of July leafless already, their leaves brown and sere, and latterly with blighted buds.[2] I assert that the city of to-day is a deadly peril to its inhabitants. But where is the remedy ? The municipalities can do nothing ; the essential need is the creation of green spaces covering from 20 to 50 per cent. of the superficial area of the city. It seems useless to dream of such things. The situation is appalling."

Thus in what he said I found some of those essential elements on which I had based my problem, elements on which since 1922 I have based my plans for a " Contemporary City."

*

The eight-hour day.

Then the eight hours of recreation. Here is the problem which the town planner must provide for.

The possibility of engaging in sport should be open to *every inhabitant of the city. And it should take place at the very door of his dwelling.* This is the programme of the garden city.[3]

[1] The adventurer, the constructor, the man of action and daring, disappears once his hour is come. This idea has something of sublimity. But, alas ! how different is reality : two or three worn-out neurotic generations ending up with sterility. Instead of a violent and glorious death we have an agony enduring over several generations.

[2] Already in the month of May, on the Champs Élysées, half the chestnuts lining the avenue have their leaves withered ; the buds have been unable to blossom and the tiny abortions of leaves are curled tightly up like a shrivelled hand. Only May ! What has happened to the seasons ? Is it already the autumn of the year ? Year in, year out, and unperceived by us, our lungs absorb these dangerous gases. But the martyred trees cry out, " Beware ! "

[3] In February 1925 I was on the jury of the International Competition for the extension of the city of Strasburg. There I saw an incredible example of unconscious stupidity. There was a closed competition for laying out the open areas of the ancient fortified zones. These zones are within five or ten minutes of the town, yet no competitor suggested they should be used for sport. What I said was : " These open areas ought to be purely and simply an immense gymnasium." Not at all ! On every plan submitted, in green and yellow washes, one could see the motley of shapes indicating the undulations of an English park, or the geometrical lay-out of a French garden—a sort of sham Luxembourg Gardens for the use of this Alsatian town and its nursemaids ! No award was made.

THE PALAIS-ROYAL

This is what the open spaces of our great cities might be like.

THE TUILERIES

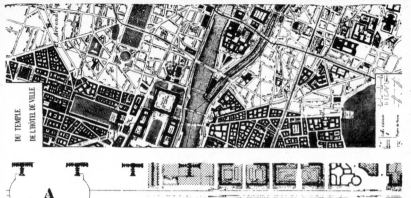

The Luxembourg.
The Palais-Royal.

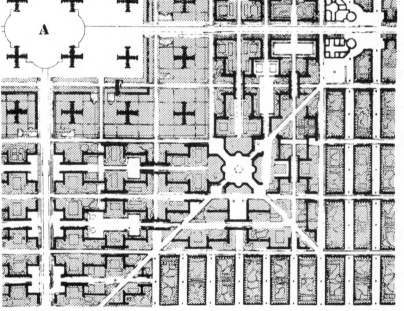

"A Contemporary City."

The skyscrapers.

The housing blocks with "set-backs."

The housing blocks on the "cellular" principle.

The Champs Élysées.
The Tuileries.

These three plans, that of the Palais-Royal district in Paris; that of the Tuileries and the Champs Élysées, and in the middle and to the same scale a fragment of the "Contemporary City," demonstrate the radical change effected in the portions built over and the open spaces: the town is literally covered with grass and trees. Compare also the width of the streets and their intersections.

Exhibition sport has nothing to do with real sport ; it is more allied to the theatre, the circus, etc. The stadium provides a spectacle where other people's marvellously developed biceps and calves can be seen. *Sport at the very door of one's house is needed,* so that everyone—men, women and children—on reaching home, can change their things and come down for play and exercise, to fill their lungs and relax and strengthen their muscles. But if it means taking a tram, a 'bus or the tube, and travelling miles with a heavy bag to carry, sport becomes impossible under such conditions. The sports ground must be at the door of the house. To bring about this Utopia the city must be built vertically. But those who regulate the architecture of Paris prohibit vertical building. They are agitating in favour of a new law which will limit the projected buildings on the wide areas reclaimed from the ancient fortifications to five storeys in place of six or seven.

It is with these confusing contradictions in mind that the town planner must approach his problem.

*

CONCERNING GARDEN CITIES

In our chapter on the Great City we saw that there were two kinds of population ; the citizens, with many good reasons for inhabiting the city proper, and the " suburbanites," those who could only live to advantage outside the city.

These suburbanites, according to their social condition, live in villas, or in dwellings in working-class quarters, or in small working-class houses which they rent.

If we formulate our problem, we shall have :

(*a*) The *present-day solution,* which exists all over the world and is looked on as ideal ; it consists of a plot of roughly 400 square yards with a little house in the middle. Part of the plot is a flower garden, and there are a few fruit trees and a tiny vegetable garden. It is complicated and difficult to keep up, and involves endless pains (call it the romantic simple life if you like) for the householder and his wife to keep things tidy, to weed it, water it, kill the slugs and the rest ; long after twilight the watering-can is still on the go. Some people may call all this a form of healthy exercise. On the contrary, it is a stupid ineffective and sometimes dangerous thing. The children

400 m²

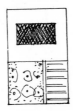

cannot play there, for they have no room to run about in, nor can the parents indulge in games or sports there. And the result of all this is a few pears and apples, a few carrots, a little parsley and so on. The whole thing is ridiculous.

400 m²

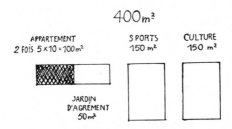

(*b*) The *suggested solution :* the dwelling occupies an area of 50 square yards and is built in two storeys, which gives 100 square yards of habitable floor space. The flower garden would take up 50 square yards. For sports I would allow 150 square yards, and for the kitchen garden another 150 square yards ; so we have our 400 square yards in full use.

The houses and their " hanging " flower gardens are juxta-posed in immense blocks " with set-backs " in three super-

A GARDEN-CITY HOUSING SCHEME ON THE CELLULAR OR
"HONEYCOMB" PRINCIPLE

The portion shown forms the entrance to the "Nouveaux Quartiers Frugès" at Bordeaux.

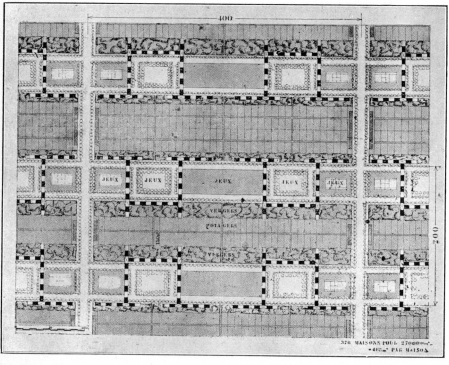

PLAN OF A GARDEN-CITY HOUSING SCHEME ON THE CELLULAR SYSTEM

Each dwelling has 100 square yards of habitable space and 50 square yards of "hanging" garden.
The blocks are constructed in three double storeys.   Every 400 yards are wide roads.

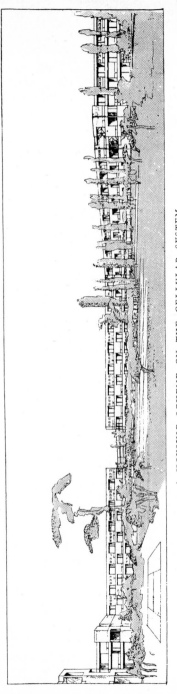

A HOUSING SCHEME ON THE CELLULAR SYSTEM

A rational utilization of the ground area. An eminently architectural solution.

imposed double storeys. The sun gets in everywhere, as does the air. The garden is paved with red tiles, its walls are hung with ivy and clematis; laurels and other shrubs cluster thickly in large cement pots ; the place is gay with flowers ; this is a real urban garden easy to keep up. There is a table sheltered from the rain where the household can eat ; one can converse or rest in the open.

At the foot of the building the 150 square yards allotted for games have been added to those of the neighbours. Football, tennis, running tracks, basket ball, etc., are all available. You come home, you change, you can take your exercise *just outside your own home.*

Close at hand are the 150 square yards of kitchen garden joined up with the similar plots belonging to the neighbours. So we get allotments of 400 yards by 100 yards, *i.e.* nearly 10 acres. The watering-can is not needed, for water is laid on ; the allotments are automatically watered and can be equally well ploughed with tractors and manured systematically.

There would be a farmer in charge of every 100 such plots and intensive cultivation would be employed. The farmer undertakes all the heavy work. The inhabitant comes back from his factory or office, and with the renewed strength given him by his games,[1] sets to work on his garden. His plot, cultivated in a standardized and scientific way, feeds him for the greater part of the year. There are storehouses on the borders of each group of plots in which he can store his produce for the winter.

Orchards lie between the houses and the cultivated ground.

In the country the eight-hour day, with its corollary of eight hours of recreation and eight hours of sleep, is gradually causing the agricultural labourer to disappear ; but this new type of housing scheme turns the inhabitant of the garden city into an agricultural labourer and *he becomes a producer.*

Here you have an example of modern town planning, where the relics of bygone days, the Swiss chalet and the like, have been relegated to the past. The mind, once it can be freed from romantic associations, will be eager to find a satisfactory solution of the problem.

The architect sees with pleasure that the notorious things we call " housing schemes " have been replaced by immense constructions on a noble scale. A sane system of communications serves, in a sensible way, these cities which are the product of a logical outlook. But I am afraid that logic is just what people find wrong with them. Garden cities have always been laid out on a basis of the poetical " simple life," with their little balconies and arches and their tiled roofs and all the other romantic paraphernalia. It is sad that thatch should not be allowed, but at least we can have artificially weathered tiles.

*

[1] It has been observed in the case of a shorthand typist, for example, that sleep is not sufficient to restore the nervous energy used up in office routine : she slowly wears herself out.

WINDING ROADS AND STRAIGHT ROADS

Twenty or thirty years ago Camillo Sitte explained to us that the straight road was a stupid thing, and the winding road the ideal. The straight road, he said, was really the longest path between two points, the winding road the shortest.; his demonstration, which was based on the maze-like cities of the Middle Ages (cities which became so by accident, see " The Pack-Donkey's Way," Chap. I),[1] was ingenious but specious. He forgot that the cities he quoted were little more than half a mile long and that their charm was the result of something quite apart from town planning. He put forward and brilliantly sustained his paradoxical argument and the fashion was set. Munich, Berlin and many other cities began to build these mazes in the very towns themselves. The English and the Germans went on planning their garden cities on the principle of the winding road, and the experiment seemed successful enough at a time when conditions were less exacting. In France we have arrived at the winding road just twenty years later, and it all looks very nice on the charmingly tinted plans of the landscape architect. In fact, winding roads in the town planner's schemes are almost a symbol in themselves of the Garden City.

The crude reality is not quite so attractive unless, as at Golders Green, the lack of design is concealed by fine old trees. This problem of the winding road in relation to garden cities deserves closer examination.

The following propositions may be admitted without a great deal of controversy.

The straight road or street is the best form for conditions of work.

---

[1] Those mediæval cities which were the result of a unified conception (such as the fortified towns) are clearly geometrical in origin. A fact which may reassure us. It would have been most upsetting to have found that the men who drew the plans and the cross-sections of the cathedrals had forsworn, in the lay-out of the towns, that clean conception which even to-day fills us with admiration (see on p 93 the plan of Montpazier).

The winding road is more appropriate for recreation.

We may also agree that the straight road gives a good sense of direction, owing to its regular transversals.

The winding road destroys all sense of direction.

And, lastly, we may admit that the straight street is eminently architectural, while the winding street is sometimes architectural.

But, if it is true that the straight road is often extremely depressing because the houses which border it are ugly, how painful is the inevitable disorder in a winding street where the houses on either side are detached. Everything then seems at sixes and sevens. The eye cannot see the curve as originally drawn on the plan, and each individual façade has its own restless importance : such housing schemes give one the impression of a field of battle or of the after-effects of an explosion.

We should also be right in saying that a straight street is extremely boring to walk through, it seems never to finish ; the pedestrian feels he is never advancing. The winding street, on the other hand, is interesting because of the variety of succeeding shapes ; we must remember this in our attempt to get the matter clear. The straight street is boring to walk in. Admitted. But if it is a street for work, then trams, 'buses and motors can get along it quickly just because it is straight.[1] Therefore let us adopt the curve if we want streets to walk in, little countrified walks, where there is no architecture, and the result will be a sort of small park or laid-out garden for promen-

[1] It is very instructive to tour through France in a motor-car. Once you get far enough from the towns you feel on solid ground again, far from the city's unbelievable follies. The main roads stretch straight to the horizon, leading quite definitely from one point to another. It was Colbert who for the most part settled their course, and after him Napoleon. Here and there a great Obelisk testifies to this. You cross over, or journey alongside, perfectly straight canals with their straight locks. On either side of your road there branch off the winding roads for special purposes—roads for cattle, donkey tracks, roads for horses and for every imaginable thing. On the one hand there is a clear and definite intention, and on the other a rather clumsy compromise. We might compare it with the sap which rises straight up the tree and the casual way (though this is more apparent than real) in which the branches stretch out towards the light. On this immense country of France, which once was forest and scrub, a human system moulded to our needs has been imposed.

aders and nursemaids. *The curved street has every justification for itself if no architectural effect is aimed at, and if the surrounding countryside, or at least the trees and grass, are picturesque and not overborne by any striking creation of man.* Clearly we are dealing in this case with roads for strolling in or walks winding through a garden city.

Finally, let us inquire if we can impose an architectural character on the winding street. Yes, if at regular intervals trees are planted, making a sort of wall. The repetition of the tree trunks makes a sort of colonnade and the branches a sort of roof. Thus the eye observes a definite geometrical form, clearly formulated. But woe to the architect who tries to line this curve with the façades of his cottages : at once an impression of disorder is created, the eye being unable to realize the beautiful curve of the landscape architect. For it does not see the street, but only the fronts of these incongruously aligned houses. If they were in front of the architect on his desk, the first thing he would do would be to try to align them better and to group them in rectangular blocks.

When the road winds, the eye can perceive but vaguely the foreshortened view. Therefore arrange the houses on either side of your winding road (so pleasant to ramble in) in blocks at right angles to each other. Standing free against the sky they make the view (as the eye sees it), which then becomes an ordered thing.

(The above theory applies to level ground. On varying levels the curve has prior rights, since here it is a question of climbing evenly by winding about : to aim at the picturesque in such a case is fatal, and the architect's problem is how to discipline the natural disorder and bring about that unity which is indispensable to every feeling of harmony and æsthetic.)

Yet the architect can create agreeable effects with curving streets by building continuous façades along them ; for thus he would create forms eminently plastic, though their frequent repetition would quickly end in boring the observer. But in towns a road of this sort, which makes it impossible to see any

distance ahead, would quickly paralyze all traffic. In garden cities the object, as far as is possible, is to avoid long rows of houses because of their many drawbacks ; for the sites are small and this involves a lack of privacy.

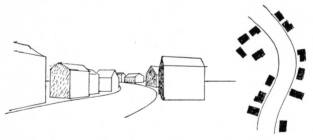

To sum up the whole matter, the curving street is essentially picturesque. Picturesqueness is a pleasure which quickly becomes boring if too frequently gratified.

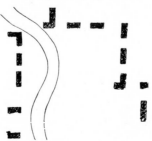

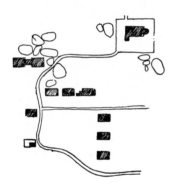

A BRETON VILLAGE (PLOUMANA CH)

The street curves amid the rectangular alignment of the houses. The direction of the prevailing wind determines the orientation of all the houses. This uniformity is pleasant.

FREEDOM THROUGH ORDER

We live in flats. A flat is a collection of mechanical and architectural elements which give us comfort and security. In terms of town planning, the flat may be considered as a cell. Cells, as a consequence of our social order, are subject to various forms of grouping, to co-operations or to antagonisms which are an essential part of the urban phenomenon. In general, we feel free in our own cell (and our dream is to live in a detached house somewhere in order to feel absolutely free), and reality teaches us that the grouping of cells attacks our freedom and so we dream of a detached house. Our crowded communal life is imposed on us by the very fact of there being towns, a fact which cannot be avoided ; and as

SAN FRANCISCO

A curving road for which the reason is obvious.   A ramp for motors.

this interference with our liberty affects our happiness, we dream (though fruitlessly) of breaking through this collective pheno-menon of which we are the slaves.

It is possible by a logically conceived ordering of these cells to attain freedom through order.

For a long time I had been anxious to formulate certain fundamental truths regarding the cell, involving a reform of the flat and its construction. Little by little, and basing each point on cause and effect, I built up an ordered system of the grouping of such cells as would replace with advantage the present chaos to which we are subject.

Let us define this modern slavery.

Your " number " for the 'bus (the number you tear off the block attached to the lamp-post) [1] is a perfect example of modern freedom as a result of order. You may be weak or helpless, a porter or a boxer, but all the same you will get the seat in the 'bus to which you are entitled. Remember how often liberty was abused before this innovation.

If we consider the general incoherence of our ordinary surroundings of to-day it is easy to see how much that *liberty* (a word rather than a reality) which is so passionately pursued by the " Parisian " is merely a snare, an obsession which covers something that grows weaker day by day. [2]

The first poor devil to be considered is the concierge in his tiny box of a room, with its deadly atmosphere ; a guardian who does pretty much as he likes. Either you are free to behave as you will, or you are perpetually badgered by that harpy his wife, " la concierge " ; it all depends on how you get on with her ; and when your visitors call they can't find her to direct them to you. Either she has gone out or she is cleaning the stairs ; in any case she is invisible.

[1] At every 'bus stop in Paris the lamp-post has attached to it a block of numbered tickets. Intending travellers tear off one and are then admitted to the 'buses in their proper turn. An example that might well be followed here for rush-hour scrambles.—F. E.

[2] I say " Parisian " because the true-blue Parisian puts up with everything with a smile. He lives in damp old houses, there is no bathroom, no hot water because it is almost impossible to install it; the staircase is dark, and the kitchen almost non-existent, and there is no electricity. He heats his flat with briquettes which grill his face and freeze his back and shed black soot over everything. Still he has a little garden on his window-sill, and the house opposite, quite as old as his own, has some admirable wrought-iron work. He is so philosophical. And Paris—charming Paris !—offers him so many distractions, with the result that he gets home late and ignores to some extent his lack of comfort. Not having any comfort, and not being difficult to please, he is delighted with everything; he feels free, they tell him so all the time in his newspapers, and proclaim it in all the Revues. It is a state of life. It is a philosophy. *All's well, I'm free !* So is the Seine. It overflows once a year and inundates thousands of worthy folk. All's well, we're free, and so is the Seine ! And so it goes on. And then there is the other type of Parisian who lives in a cosy apartment in a new building, in a wide avenue, with lift and bathroom and carpeted stairs. He too loves *ancient Paris*, her crumbling walls and wrought iron. He too has been touched by this religion, inculcated in the Press and on the Stage, of the value of individual liberty in Paris.

And when you do get in, you hope for peace at last. And at once the gramophone or the piano begins ; or else there is a babel of noise below or above, and on every hand you are sandwiched between three or four neighbours ; you are like a currant in a pudding. In general the staircase is none too commodious and is badly lit. Naturally there is no lift. If you have any servants, they are housed uncomfortably somewhere under the roof, in close and often inadvisable proximity to others. And once we get on to the subject of servants, we begin to see how really free we are ! One day a week we have to do for ourselves. If you like company of an evening, your servants sulk, and there is a domestic crisis. Perhaps you want to give a party. Where are you to give it ? In your drawing-room ? It is rather small and your neighbours expect to be able to go to sleep about ten. So that in your free Paris you can have a party exactly twice a year ; once at the feast of *Saint-Sylvestre* in your own house, and once on the 14th of July in the street, As for physical culture, it takes you an hour to get to the gymnasium and you are charged heavily ; so you don't go because it is too difficult. You do exercises instead in your own bedroom. This needs a will of iron, and you give up after about the third morning, finding you have overslept : that is the end of physical culture for you.

As for food, your maid goes to the local store and wastes a lot of time, and everything is very expensive. As for your car, the garage is ten minutes away, and if it is raining you reach home soaked, in spite of having a car. And your children have to be taken to the Park to play : that is, if they have a nurse-maid or governess.

What if we could at one step wipe out all these difficulties ? What if we could utilize, moreover, new ideas and improve matters to make life pleasanter ! If expenses could be reduced : if we could be relieved of nearly all our domestic worries : if, by setting things in order, we could assure a maximum of domestic liberty and *by order bring about freedom :* if this modern slavery could be done away with !

Let us analyze the needs of the family (*i.e.* a "cell"): also, what is necessary for a given number of such cells in their mutual relation to each other, and let us see how many cells can usefully be combined together to make a manageable colony in the way an hotel or a village is manageable; a community which would be a clear organic unit in the urban scheme, a definite thing having a well-defined function involving a close examination into strict necessities and a clear statement of the problem. So let us state our problem, and after due deliberation we shall hit on a formula which must answer to a good many requirements: as liberty; amenities; beauty; economy in construction; low cost: bodily health; harmonious functioning of vital organs; and a useful contribution to the many urban problems such as traffic, fresh air, police, etc.

Let us go a little more fully into the scheme for dwellings on the "honeycomb" or cellular principle, or "freehold maisonnettes." [1]

The site measures 400 × 200 yards, for this is the best dimension for the intersection of streets (see p. 222). The houses have their backs to the street and look out on open spaces 300 × 120 square yards in area (nearly ten acres). There are no internal courtyards or wells. Every flat is in reality a house of two storeys, a sort of villa with its own garden: this applies to every double-storey. This garden is a cell 18 feet in height by 27 feet wide by 21 feet deep, ventilated by a great well 15 yards square in section: each of these cells acts as a ventilator and the building resembles an immense sponge for the absorption of air: the whole building breathes. The great park is at the foot of the block of flats and is reached by six underground passages; there are a football ground, two tennis-courts, three open spaces for other games, a clubhouse, woods and lawns. The "roadway" is not merely for motors, it is continued vertically by means of vast staircases (with lifts and goods lifts) each serving 100 to 150 maisonnettes; and its use is extended at

---

[1] An early form of this scheme was shown at the Salon d'Automne, 1922, and developed in *Towards a New Architecture*, 1926.

various levels by means of footbridges which cross the road and become a part of the corridors on to which the doors of the maisonnettes open. Behind each such door is a maisonnette. Each of these forms a perfect cube, and each is totally independent of its neighbour, being separated one from the other by the " hanging " gardens. The street also continues into the garage, which is both at and under pavement level : each maisonette has its own garage. This roadway is constructed entirely of concrete and is used only by light motor traffic. It is *raised* on piles. Heavy lorries and 'buses run below, *at ground level*, and the lorries have direct access to the storerooms of the buildings which form the ground floor : in this way we eliminate that disastrous pulling up by the curb which blocks the streets and makes even pedestrian progress difficult. All the service mains are get-at-able and the navvy's doom is sealed. On the roof of the building there is a 1000-yard track on which to run in the fresh air, and there also are the gymnasiums, where instructors would direct parents as well as children; there are sun parlours too, which have proved so successful in the United States in combating tuberculosis. There would also be reception-rooms where friends could now and then be entertained in a pleasant and dignified fashion. The concierge has vanished. Instead of the large number of these needed at the present time, six men-servants would suffice working in eight-hour shifts. Day and night they would be in charge of the block, each in a magnificent entrance hall 100 feet long, set over and across the two-storey roadway ; receiving visitors, announcing them by telephone and directing them to the right lifts : on these roadways traffic would be one-way and the pedestrian would not need to cross the road to enter the building.

The plans and sections given here show a logical arrangement of all these elements ; by attaining order we arrive at liberty.

The most rigorous standards govern the whole building down to the smallest detail; the standardization of the builder's yard finds its most uncompromising application here.

The idea of grouping 660 flats, which means from 3,000 to 4,000 inhabitants, in such a block of closed cell-like elements is to make of them a sort of community, the creation of which would bring about freedom through order. There would be six staircase wells and six entrance halls to serve the 660 flats on the five storeys, all of which things are at present permitted by the building regulations of Paris. But if it could be built six storeys high there would be 792 flats and seven storeys would give 924 flats.

The ground-floor of these housing blocks would form an immense workshop for household economy : here are the commissariat, the restaurant service, domestic service and laundering.

We have seen how the street system is continued from the upper and lower levels to the door of each villa, but the plans show also another system—this time vertical—which gives access to every storey from basement to roof, thus connecting the workshop on the ground-floor with the service corridor to each maisonnette. By this means all the organisation of domestic economy in these " cellular " apartments takes place.

A co-operative organization or hotel syndicate could direct the catering and domestic service.

As for the commissariat, provisions are bought wholesale direct from the country—meat, game, vegetables, fruit—and are placed in cold storage on the ground floor. This would give a saving of 30 to 40 per cent. as against the prices charged at the great stores. (I leave to those interested the problem of what will happen to the Central Markets under such a system.) The kitchen would be capable of supplying meals of a simple or elaborate sort at all hours. If you desired to bring some friends back to supper round about midnight, say after the theatre, a mere telephone call is all that is needed for you to find the table laid and waiting for you—with a servant who is not sulking, as he happens to have just come on for the night shift. An experienced hotel manager, a specialist with a staff of specialists, would organize and see to the whole domestic

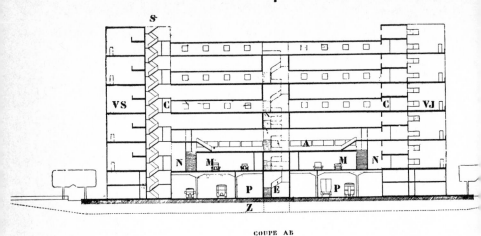

COUPE AB

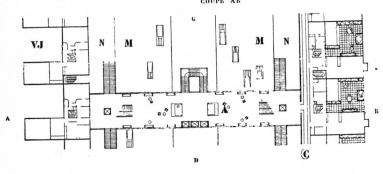

3

BLOCKS OF DWELLINGS ON THE " CELLULAR " SYSTEM

Fig. 1.—*Vertical section taken across the street and showing the stair wells, the suspended bridges and the " hanging gardens."*

Fig. 3.—*Plan taken at the level of the entrance hall which bridges the street. To left and right are the blocks of dwellings separated by the street, which is 150 feet wide ; then come the pavements with the stairs giving access to the hall, then the two one-way streets ; in the centre are the roofs of the garages.*

A. *Hall.*
E. *The main staircase, lifts, goods lift.*
C. *Corridors on to which the " villas " open.*
VJ. *A " hanging garden."*
VS. *A living-room.*
N. *Pavement and stairs giving access to the hall.*
M. *Roadway raised on piles for light traffic.*
P. *Roadways at ground level for heavy traffic.*
Z. *Subterranean passage leading to the enclosed parks or gardens.*
R. *Internal parks or gardens.*
S. *Solaria (under " S " one of the service stairs is seen).*

2

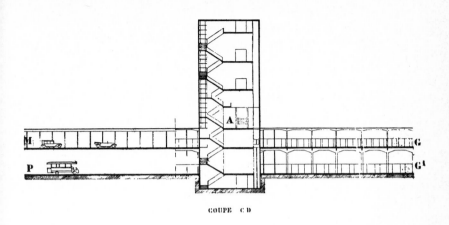

COUPE C D

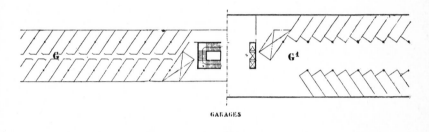

GARAGES

4

BLOCKS OF DWELLINGS ON THE "CELLULAR" SYSTEM

Fig. 2.—Longitudinal section parallel to the street and main staircase.

Fig. 4.—Plan. To the left are the garages opening on the higher street level ; to the right the lower range of garages situated at ground level. G^1 is connected with G by a motor lift. From G and G^1 communication is direct with the main staircase (E) and the hall (A) and consequently with the "villas" themselves.

economy of the block. Any cleaning would be carried out by
professional cleaners, and you would be spared the sulks of the
maid when a little extra polishing has to be done.   But even if
the whole service of your apartment is taken over by an organization such as I have outlined above, it will still always be
possible to have a maid or children's nurse of your own, a family
servant, should you so wish. At any rate the servant problem
will be solved for you, and that is no slight contribution to
your daily peace : you will have acquired freedom through
order.

Under the present conditions which govern our cities,
everything is in confusion and at odds, nothing is really properly
arranged.   If things are once put into shape and order we shall
be able to appreciate the calm joys of freedom.   Family life
could be lived in peace and the bachelor would not have the last
word.

ON REPETITION OR MASS PRODUCTION

In previous chapters of this book I have dealt with æsthetics
and economics. with the attainment of perfection and with the
modern spirit ; and one prime necessity emerges clearly :

WE MUST BUILD ON A CLEAR SITE. *The city of to-day is dying
because it is not constructed geometrically.   To build on a clear site is
to replace the " accidental " lay-out of the ground, the only one that
exists to-day, by the formal lay-out.   Otherwise nothing can save us.
And the consequence of geometrical plans is Repetition and Mass-
production.*

And as a consequence of repetition, the *standard* is created,
and so perfection (the creation of types).

Repetition dominates everything. We are unable to produce industrially at normal prices without it ; it is impossible
to solve the housing problem without it.   The builders' yard
must become a workshop with a proper staff and machinery and
specialized gangs.   The vagaries of weather and seasons can
then be ignored.   " Building " must cut out its " off seasons."

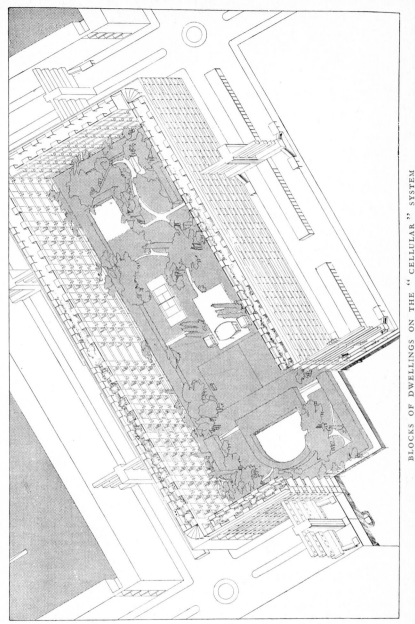

BLOCKS OF DWELLINGS ON THE " CELLULAR " SYSTEM

Axonometric perspective of a complete unit.
The height of the buildings is roughly 110 feet above ground level.

221

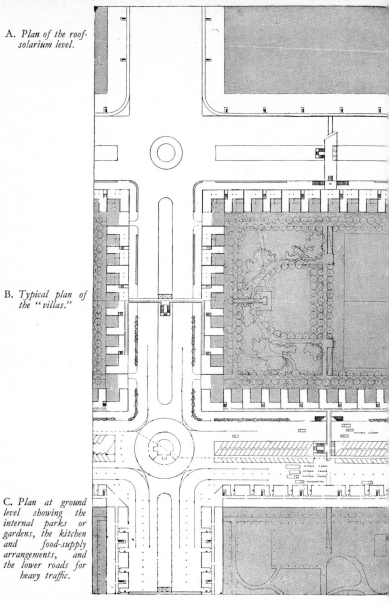

A. *Plan of the roof-solarium level.*

B. *Typical plan of the "villas."*

C. *Plan at ground level showing the internal parks or gardens, the kitchen and food-supply arrangements, and the lower roads for heavy traffic.*

BLOCKS OF DWELLINGS ON THE CELLULAR OR "HONEYCOMB" SYSTEM

(Composite plan of a complete block occupying an area of 400 × 200 *yards.)*

A. *Showing the service stairs, each serving a vertical section of two apartments and giving on to solarium and running track.*

B. *Showing the way in which the "hanging gardens" are ventilated, and the way the flats are lin. up by a system of corridors and main stairs with the garages, halls and the two sup. imposed streets.*

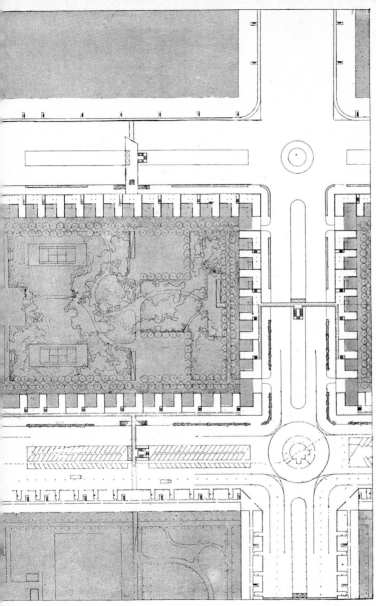

Showing the double-storeyed ground floor, for the domestic and supply organizations: re-
frigerators, shops, stores, kitchens, restaurants, laundries, domestic services, administration,
etc.

e open spaces (i.e. gardens, etc.) amount to 48 per cent. of the total area of the site. If the
"hanging gardens" are added, the open spaces amount to 90 per cent.

be density of population is 120 *persons to the acre. The average density in Paris to-day is* 145.

BLOCKS OF DWELLINGS ON THE CELLULAR SYSTEM. PART OF
A FAÇADE

*The restricted floor to floor unit in present-day façades is about 11 feet; this
is increased to nearly 20 feet, resulting in a nobler scale altogether in the architecture of the street.*

A PORTION OF A "SOLARIUM" ON THE ROOF OF A PRIVATE
HOUSE AT AUTEUIL

Built 1924.

BLOCKS OF DWELLINGS ON THE CELLULAR OR "HONEYCOMB" SYSTEM

One of the "hanging gardens" to each flat, 15, 30 or 60 feet above the ground. (Shown at the Esprit Nouveau Pavilion at the Exhibition of Decorative Art, Paris, 1925.)

Without making any claims in regard to their intrinsic value, we may honestly admit that the Plans I have put forward in support of the conception of my " cellular " system for dwellings anticipate the problem of mass-production. The

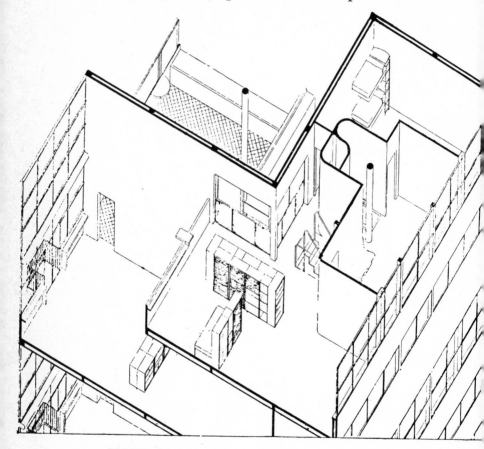

BLOCKS OF DWELLINGS ON THE CELLULAR SYSTEM

Axonometric section and perspective of a " villa." Standardization is the keynote in every element of the construction. This unit was worked out minutely and shown in the Pavilion of the Esprit Nouveau at the International Exhibition of Decorative Arts, Paris, 1925.

1915.   A " DOMINO " HOUSE

A standardized framework or " skeleton " designed for mass-production.

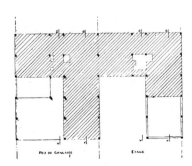

1922.   A " CITROHAN " HOUSE

*Model shown at the Salon d'Automne.   Standardization of all elements (the
framework, doors and windows).*

BLOCK OF VILLAS

*Design shown at the Salon d'Automne.   The builder's yard becomes indus-
trialized as the result of a comprehensive standardization.*

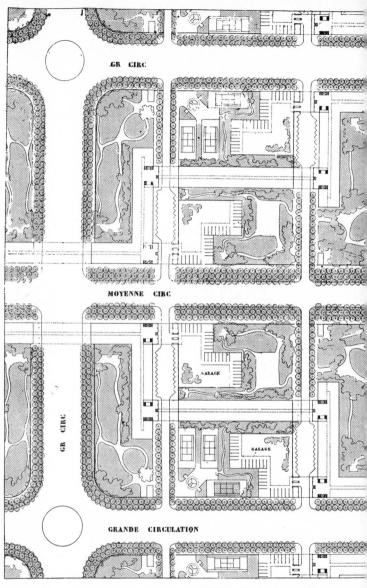

GR CIRC

MOYENNE CIRC

GR CIRC

GARAGE

GARAGE

GRANDE CIRCULATION

DWELLINGS WITH " SET-BAC

In this plan the main arteries are shown as 150 feet in width, and forming s
large island sites thus formed could be enclosed by railings. Leading right up ꞏ
garage (G). There are gardens and parks everywhere. The amount of ground
The density of population is 120 persons to the acre as against 145 in Paris to-

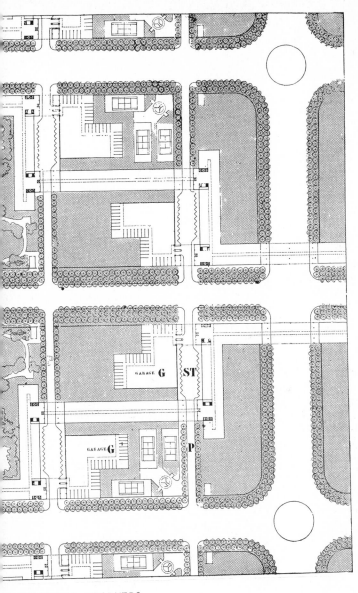

RESIDENTIAL QUARTERS

s 400 × 600 yards in area. Every 200 yards lesser streets cccur. The
nces are private roads with parking places for cars (ST). Each flat has its own
ilt over is 15 per cent. of the total area, leaving 85 per cent. of open space.

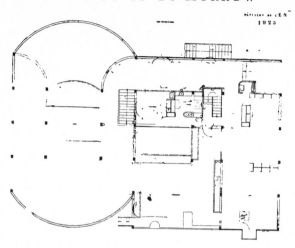

1924–25. PLAN OF THE PAVILION OF THE ESPRIT NOUVEAU AT THE EXHIBITION OF DECORATIVE ARTS

To the left the pavilion containing the panoramas which embody a scheme of town planning for a city containing 3,000,000 inhabitants, i.e the " Voisin " plan for Paris ; and on the right a complete unit in a block of " Villas," formed entirely of standardized elements.

1925. A SKETCH OF THE PAVILION OF THE ESPRIT NOUVEAU

It was formally opened by M. de Monzie, Minister in the Cabinet, on July 10th, 1925. He said : " In my capacity as Representative of the Government, I wish to testify to the interest it takes in all efforts such as this ; no Government can afford to ignore the work that is being done here."

classification which is inherent in it and the precise determining of the various functions can only result, after much experiment, in bringing about the realization of types which are genuinely *pure*. By breaking down first one thing and then another, every difficulty may be vanquished little by little and a functional and sane urban architecture will come into being.

If only our captains of industry would examine these plans they would see immense scope in these suggestions. Industry could then devote itself to " building," and the urban environment in which we work and rest would be transformed.

We must never, in our studies, lose sight of the purely human " cell," the cell which responds most perfectly to our physiological and sentimental needs. We must arrive at the "housemachine," which must be both practical and emotionally satisfying and designed for a succession of tenants. The idea of the " old home " disappears, and with it local architecture, etc., for labour will shift about as needed, and must be ready to move, *bag and baggage*. The words " bag and baggage " will do very well to express the kind—the " type "—of furniture needed. Standardized houses with standardized furniture.[1] Everything is already in a ferment, ideas meet and clash round this very point, which has sprung from a real feeling even before it has been enunciated clearly. Already, with a view to the standardization of building, proposals have been made for founding an international organization to lay down building " standards." [2]

---

[1] See *Towards a New Architecture*, published by Rodker, London, and *L'Art decoratif d'aujourd'hui*, published by Crés, Paris.

[2] The Pavilion of the *Esprit Nouveau* at the Paris Exhibition of Decorative Arts in 1925 constituted in itself a document of standardization. All its furnishings were the product of industry and not of the decorators. The building itself was a " cell " in a block of flats, a unit in a housing scheme, built on the " honeycomb " principle.

When I submitted my scheme in January 1924 to the architects-in-chief to the Exhibition, it was categorically rejected. They wished me to illustrate the theme " An Architect's House." I answered, " No, I will do a house for everybody, or, if you prefer it, the apartment of any gentleman who would like to be comfortable in beautiful surroundings."

The difference of opinion was complete. The Pavilion was as it were smuggled in, no jury considered it, and we had no grant towards building it. What difficulties we experienced !

THE URBAN SCENE

We rarely care to look at the silhouette of houses seen against the sky; the sight would be too painful. Throughout the town, in every street, the silhouette seems like a gash, a ragged, tumultuous line with jutting broken forms. And our need of delight and of enthusiasm finds nothing to evoke it in this incoherence. Our emotion would be of a very different kind if the profile of the town seen against the sky were pure and made us feel it was the result of some potent ordering mind. Garret windows, tiles and gutters crown our cities, and occupy in the urban scheme that privileged position where the two determining constants of all optical sensation—the perpendicular and the horizontal—intersect.

Reinforced concrete provides a solution—a revolution of the scheme of things whereby the " roof " (a jumble of garret windows, tiles and gutters) has always been treated as a sort of "no man's land," haunted only by Louis Wain's cats. It now becomes an immense reclaimed surface, a superficial area of the city available for gardens or walks. To put it poetically, the gardens of Semiramis have come to us; they are realizable and have been realized; they astonish and delight us, they are useful and they are beautiful ! The profile of the town seen against the sky becomes a pure line, and as a result we are able to lay out our urban scene on the grand scale. This is of the first importance. I repeat that the silhouette against the sky is a determining factor in our feelings; it is exactly the same thing as profile and contour in sculpture.

I may say at once that even if this purity of the city's silhouette is regained it will be useless if the corridor-street is to remain. We must break up the corridor-street and, properly speaking, we must create the *broad vista* in the urban scene. That must be our aim, and not the monotony of the narrow depth which the corridor-street gives us. In designing my Blocks of Dwellings with " set-backs," I have provided wide vistas to right and to left, and by constantly getting back to

CHICAGO

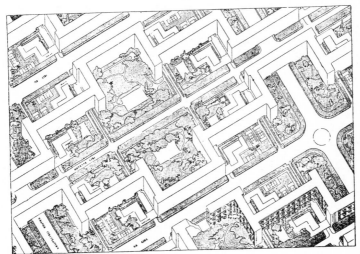

DWELLINGS
WITH
"SET-BACKS

*But people will say : " Your proposals will end in the horrors of the typical
American town with its mechanical lay-out." Here is a comparison.*

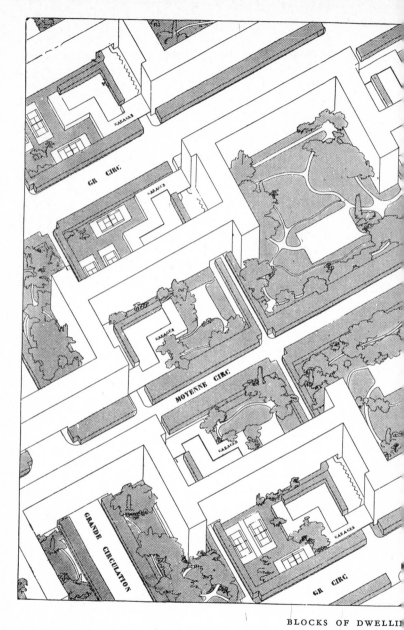

Labels within the image: GR CIRC · GR CIRC · MOYENNE CIRC · GRANDE CIRCULATION · GARAGES

An axonometric perspective.   Thanks to the access of light and air which the " cellul
courtyards are altogether eliminated.
By a special arrangement of great importance, under which the " villas " are grouped
maisonnettes, i.e. twelve storeys.   This arrangement can be seen in the portion shou

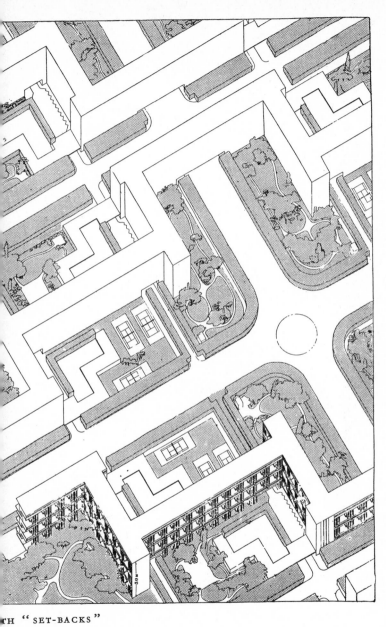

'H " SET-BACKS "

'em makes possible, the depth of each block can be as much as 65 feet, though internal

'cuncial fashion, three corridors suffice to give access to every six levels of the
'ion at the bottom right-hand corner of the plate.

the longitudinal axis my composition takes on an architectural character ; the hitherto dull lines of the corridor-street now become a series of prism forms which give emphasis to the recesses or to the projections ; and the depressing façades of the corridor have been replaced by geometrical shapes juxtaposed, or set far apart, or brought together in a monumental and lively urban landscape.

This new lay-out enables us to introduce trees into our city. Leaving hygienic considerations on one side for the moment, it may be admitted, æsthetically speaking, that the proximity of geometrical forms of dwellings to the picturesque forms of vegetation produces a much-needed and satisfying combination in our urban scene. Indeed, having got so far with our rich variety of plastic forms, the clear-cut shapes of the buildings, the rounded forms of the foliage and the arabesques of the branches, hardly anything remains to be done except to continue to develop these good things. To illustrate what I mean I will give a concrete example. The *Tuileries* might be continued over whole quarters of Paris in the form of parks, whether of the formal French kind or in the undulating English manner, and could be combined with purely geometrical architecture. I conclude with this reassuring statement : no matter how rigidly uniform the façades of our dwellings with " set-backs " may be, they will form a sort of grill or trellis against which the trees will display themselves to advantage, and this whether they are seen close at hand or from a distance ; they will make a sort of draught-board which will harmonize well with the formal flower-beds. To go back to the conclusions of an earlier chapter : uniformity in detail is at the base of all architectural practice ; but uniformity in detail implies variety in the general effect. The problem is now put on a wider basis : the house is no longer a fraction of façade 50 or 75 feet in length, it extends to 600 or 1,200 feet, and it is varied by the lively incidence of its recessions and salients. Think of the Procuracies, the Place des Vosges or the Place Vendôme, and it will be clear that the architectural " frills " of these famous places are not for one moment their only claim to beauty. And the economist will conclude : Here is a plan which permits us to standardize building by a full use of machinery, industrial organization and the creation of standards. Out of the earth spring up the shrubs and foliage, the lawns stretch away into the distance, and the beds of flowering plants. A ring of geometrical forms encloses this charming and picturesque scene, and the silhouette seen against the sky is an architectural one. The old corridor-street has given way to wide, noble and cheerful spaces.

*

THE HUMAN SCALE

Now, all these considerations apply to functions which appertain to *man* and man's height varies between, say, 5 feet 6 inches and 6 feet 2 inches. And when man finds himself alone in vast empty spaces he grows disheartened. We must learn how to tighten up the urban landscape and discover units of measurement to our own scale. This problem is essentially one of architecture. Architecture is able to make great play with contrasts, to harmonize simple elements with complex ones and small with great, to blend the forcible with the graceful. The vast buildings which the town planning of the future will bring about would crush us if there were no common measure between them and ourselves. We have already seen how a tree is a thing that pleases us all, since, however remotely, we are still children of Nature ; and we have seen that an urban mani-festation which completely ignored Nature would soon find itself at odds with our deepest primeval impulses. The tree modifies a scene that is too vast, and its casual forms contrast with the rigid forms which we have conceived and made by the machinery of our epoch. It would seem that the tree is an element essential to our comfort, and its presence in the city is a sort of caress, a kindly thing in the midst of our severe creations.

Nor must we ignore the need we have all felt at times of reducing the scale of the urban scene, so that we can elbow one another, move in crowds, and see one another at close quarters. Thus the human scale must always be the ultimate factor in the mind of the architect who has to design the immense blocks of buildings which are necessitated by practical and financial considerations. There must never come a time when people can be bored in our city.

Though the sky-scrapers rise to a height of over 600 feet, yet between them and in the midst of the great open spaces there would be boulevards bordered by buildings not more

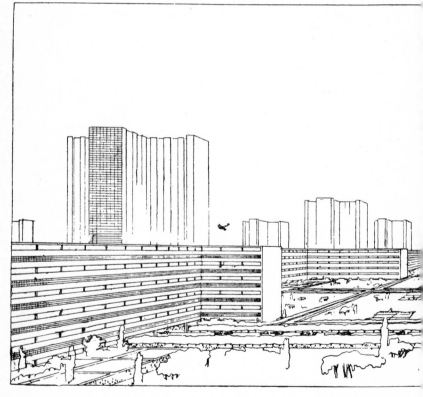

View showing a large housing scheme with " set-backs."   The buildings are six do from the " corridor-street."   Every window of e

than three storeys high and with receding stages.   These would house the luxury shops, and there too would be the restaurants and cafés on the various terraces, giving on to alleys of trees or the great parks.   The street would thus be reorganized on a human scale.   In this City of Sky-scrapers we should, in fact, be able to restore just that very scale which is really in conformity with our own dimensions : the one-storeyed house.

And so my scheme, which at first glance might seem to warrant a certain fear and dislike, brings us back to something

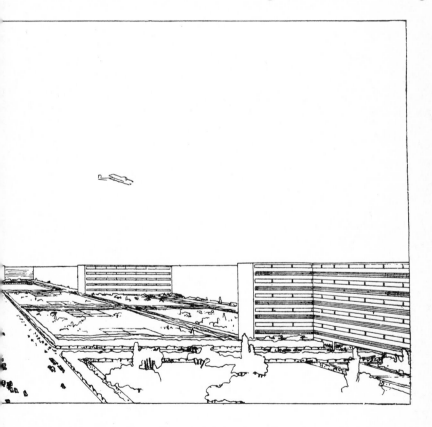

...s in height.   The " set-backs " supply an architectural motive which takes us far (and that on both frontages) looks on to open spaces.

we have had to forgo with regret in towns of the nineteenth century : architecture to our own scale.

We are fond of the crowd and the crush because we are human beings and like to live in groups. In such a town as I have outlined, with a denser population than that of any existing cities, there would be ample provision and opportunity for close human contact ; there would be trees, flowers and spreading lawns, and one-storey houses with receding terraces, for the eye to feed on. What would it matter if beyond these " consoling " elements and behind the screen of trees there stood the tremendous silhouettes of the sky-scrapers ? They would supply a background bathed in light, radiant with their glazed façades, for though they are of enormous size, they have nothing in common with the overwhelming heavy masses that stifle and oppress New York. What would it matter if in the dwellings with " set-backs " the terraces rose to a height of 120 feet, if the architectural contour was ample and beautiful and formed a pure silhouette against the abundant foliage ?

On a human scale ? The answer lies in the proper enuncia-tion of the problem ; we must get the trees back into the city and create an urban lay-out infinitely more varied than the corridor-streets which have hitherto been such a depressing element in our lives.

*

PRIDE

Pride makes us pull ourselves together and look things in the face. In place of depression and weakness it gives us a new energy and strength : it makes for keenness and activity as against indifference and listlessness. It is a powerful lever. Pride is neither arrogance nor vanity.

There are times when a common civic pride informs the masses with faith and activity : and we are compelled to admit that it is at those moments when faith inspires action that the best periods come into being. They spring from action (some-times from *one* simple event), and they inspire action in the

form of enterprise, invention, initiative and new ideas. It is then
that great things get accomplished, for a special state of mind
is brought about which is able to influence every department
of human activity, and the result is a spiritual structure that has
a social side as well as a material one. Beauty, which as it were
waits upon creative powers, becomes incarnate in some new
creation. Beauty, which is born of action, inspires enthusiasm
and provokes men to action. And there have been periods in
which fortunate peoples have found themselves sustained and
raised by civic pride to a higher level than their wont.

Such moments can only arise when the diverse ways, in
which the collective effort takes place, happen to meet ; a
moment where all solutions seem to have been simultaneously
hit upon, and where a universal crystallization seems to take
place. And this can happen quickly, violently, almost un-
expectedly, once the preliminary steps are completed.

The chemistry of crowds is as exact as that of metals ; the
formula needs its exact valencies before an answer can be
given. We use the words " the melting-pot of a period " so
easily because we feel within us the invisible transmutation
into terms of mathematics of those valencies which are about
to precipitate the pure metal.

When amid all the confusion and stir, all the seemingly
disordered movement that surrounds us, we begin to see a few
gleams of light and signs of constructiveness, then we can begin
to feel that the moment of crystallization is close at hand. If
these indications have set immense numbers of people in motion,
if these ideas (moral, social or technical) are right, then we are
justified in believing that a great age is upon us and will show
itself in noble accomplishments. If we could formulate clearly
what it is we expect, if clear formulas could be attained which
would everywhere explain and set forth the general trend, then
we should merely have to wait for the right moment to solve
the problem. And when some day, arising from all sorts of
opposite directions, and from every kind of environment, the
same mode of thinking brings about a commonly accepted

system, a clear and radiant harmony will be the result. In that glowing and harmonious moment of construction and enthusiasm, pride will be born and satisfaction in achievements adequately conceived and capable of development and grandeur.

Civic pride becomes incarnate in the material achievements of architecture. The ages have successively established the periods of architecture. Santa Maria dei Fiori at Florence, the marble pavements of Venice, the Parthenon and the cathedrals were all created by republics animated by civic pride. And do you suppose that Americans have no pride—even though a little questionably—in the sight of the gigantic Manhattan sky-scrapers as they stand up from the sea ?

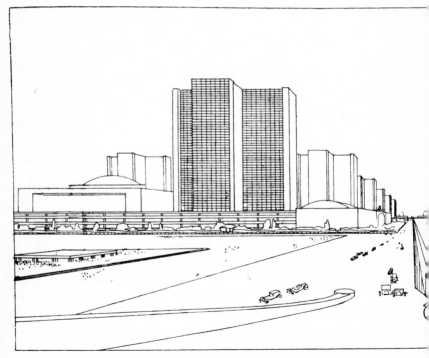

A CONTEMPORARY CI

The city seen from one of the main tracks for fast motor traffic.   To left and right the Of
scrapers are shown grouped toge

A collective enthusiasm animates men's gestures, ideas, decisions and their acts. It results in material works, and it is that very passion, expressed in plastic terms and involving both precision and the capacity to move us, that marks the style of an epoch. For style—where plastic forms are used—is a creation of the mind and therefore passion. Passion, fire, ardour, faith, rapture, animation, all lead to happiness.

If we do not produce, we die. If we do not act, the world does not merely mark time; it grows enfeebled and goes to pieces, with the inevitable results of famine and a reversion to barbarism. Movement is the law of our existence: nothing ever stands still, for if it does it begins to go backwards and is

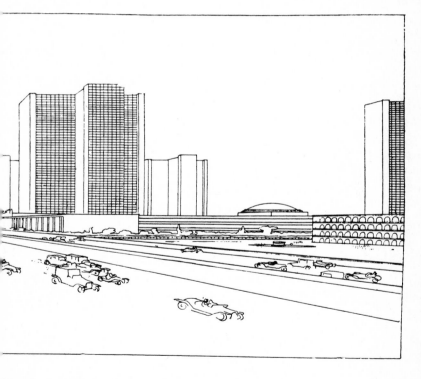

blic Services. Further in the background the Museums and Universities. The sky-
athed in light and air.

destroyed, and this is the very definition of life. Therefore we must act, we must advance, we must produce. After a century and a half of miraculous preparation, reason has come into her own in company with science, and science has flung us violently into the machine age. Everything is revolutionized. It seemed as though progress could lead to nothing but universal destruction, but all that crumbled was the old world. Through the debris the new world began to appear boldly. Reason alone, which appeared definitely to dominate everything, might have led us into the deepest despair, but the violent forces of life seem to have thrust us once more into a new adventure. Reason and passion join hands to produce something constructive. A whole way of thinking lies there, and its natural result will be a style. Already some clear-sighted thinkers foresee this new consciousness from which civic pride will be born—that pride which can move the masses.

Our world, like a charnel-house, is strewn with the detritus of dead epochs. The great task incumbent on us is that of making a proper environment for our existence, and clearing away from our cities the dead bones that putrefy in them. We must construct cities for to-day.

Men with tired or shocked minds resist this reasoning and invoke the fallacious wisdom of their experience. Actually they belong to yesterday and cannot see what is happening round them. The new generation is full of enthusiasm and ready to take up the task. We come at a moment between two epochs—the pre-machine age and the machine age. The machine age is not yet fully conscious of itself; it has not yet gathered its forces, nor begun to construct; it has not yet achieved that architectural style by means of which it will first of all gratify its material needs, and after that satisfy the pure sentiment which informs it; a sentiment which leads man to do well and beautifully what he has to do; that sensation of creating and ordering which is essential to his happiness.

Happiness is not a coin in the pocket nor a cake in the hand. It is a feeling, an imponderable, and it comes from the heart.

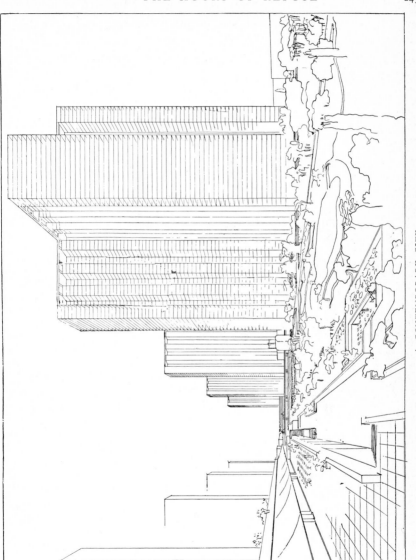

A CONTEMPORARY CITY

The parks at the base of the sky-scrapers. On the right the "set-backs." To the left the receding terraces of the restaurants, cafés, and shops. In the distance may be seen the fast motor track between two buildings, which might well be pure architectural creations

*The centre of the city seen from one of the terraced cafés surrounding the Great Central Stat
above ground level. Leaving the station the "speedway" is seen continuing to the right
of population and traffic ; there is any amount of room for both. The terraces contain
scattered in the open spaces between the sky-scrapers and are surrounded by trees.*

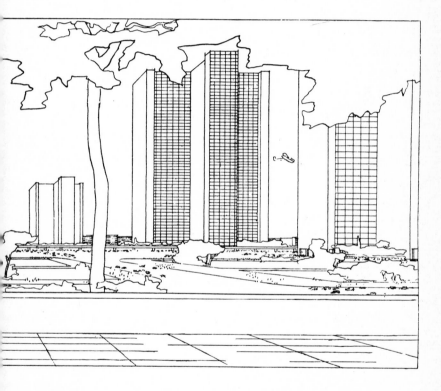

re. *The station can be seen between the two sky-scrapers on the left, only slightly raised*
direction of the Park.   We are in the very centre of the city, the point of greatest density
cafés are much frequented and serve as boulevards.   Theatres, public halls, etc., are

THIRD PART
A CONCRETE CASE: THE CENTRE OF PARIS

At the present moment, in a number of highly strategic points in Paris, great blocks of decayed and out-of-date buildings are being demolished and on their sites new buildings are being erected.

Nobody interferes. And on the site of the old city which was so destructive to life a new city is rising which will be even more deadly to life in that it is creating real centres of congestion without any modification of the street.

These financially profitable transactions in the centre of Paris are like a cancer which is permitted to settle round the heart of the city. They can only end by stifling it. To permit such a state of things to go on is an incredible act of irresponsibility at this dangerous moment through which all great cities are passing.

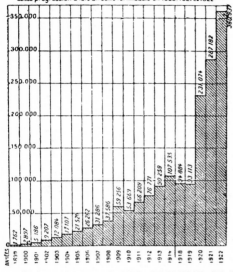

CRAPHIQUE INDIQUANT L'ACCROISSEMENT DE LA CIRCULATION DES VEHICULES
AUTOMOBILES EN FRANCE AU COURS DES VINGT-TROIS DERNIÈRES ANNÉES
Apres un léger recul durant les années de guerre
cette progression a fait un bond formidable en 1920, 1921 et 1922

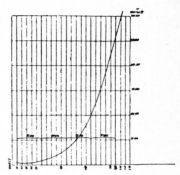

The curve shows the increase in
population.

GRAPH SHOWING THE INCREASE IN MOTOR TRAFFIC IN FRANCE
DURING THE LAST TWENTY-THREE YEARS

*There was a slight set-back during the years of the War, but the sudden increase
in 1920, 1921 and 1922 is astounding.*

XIV

PHYSIC OR SURGERY

IN 1922 the French Press was silent on the question of town
planning; in 1923 the occasional appearance of articles
devoted to this question was significant; people began to
be aware that the subject was of vital importance. In 1924
the whole Press gave tongue, so to speak, almost every day.
Town planning *had* to be considered, for Paris was sick, deadly
sick.

"Keep moving." "Keep moving." Traffic remedies are
constantly demanded and remedies are constantly proposed.

Paris is sick. And the Faculty (in this case the authorities) is divided into two camps, the physicians and the surgeons. In truth, the physicians are timid and the surgery is of a soothing kind ! Everyone is so convinced that the remedy will prove ineffectual that no proposal ever comes into effect. None the less it is of the greatest importance to us to know if physic will suffice or if the knife is inevitable.

*

We shall find the opportune solution (and by that I mean a possible solution, one which can be realized *at once* both as to material and to finance, and a profitable one for anyone who has sufficient courage to take it up) in what is at present the most dangerous and menacing cancer now beginning to strangle the city and which will end by stifling it. This cancer is the business of demolition and reconstruction which has been going on at various points in Paris for the last year or two : the actual spots themselves are extremely significant : they provide an *a priori* demonstration of the theory of the Centre of a City already put forward in Chapter VII. I shall formulate it more fully in my next chapter. It is a theory which those who go about with their eyes and ears shut qualify as folly.

AT THIS VERY MOMENT IN A NUMBER OF HIGHLY STRATEGIC POINTS IN PARIS IMMENSE BLOCKS OF DECAYED AND OUT-OF-DATE BUILDINGS ARE BEING DEMOLISHED, AND ON THEIR SITES NEW BUILDINGS AND BLOCKS OF OFFICES ARE BEING ERECTED. THE STREET IS LEFT EXACTLY AS IT WAS : OCCASIONALLY THE BUILDING LINE IS TAKEN SIX OR TWELVE FEET FURTHER BACK. NOTHING ELSE IS DONE. THESE ENTERPRISING AND PROFITABLE SPECULATIONS DEMONSTRATE MOST CLEARLY IN PRACTICE THE POSSIBILITIES OF DEMOLITION AND REBUILDING TO-DAY. BUT, ON THE OTHER HAND, THESE PROFITABLE SPECULATIONS ARE ESTABLISHING *IN THE CENTRE OF PARIS* CERTAIN FIXED POINTS WHICH WILL FORM *THE BASIS OF THE NEW TWENTIETH CENTURY CITY*. NOW THESE FIXED POINTS HAVE BEEN IN NOWISE DICTATED BY THE ACTUAL

PROBLEM OF THE LAY-OUT OF THE TOWN. IS IT NOT
STRANGE THAT UPON THE RUINS OF THE OLD CITY, WHICH
WAS SO DEADLY A THING, MEN SHOULD BE PERMITTED TO
BUILD A NEW CITY WHICH IS BOUND TO PROVE EVEN MORE

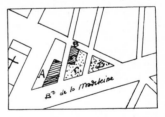

The points marked A, B, C
and D *on the plan mark the
positions of buildings to be
rebuilt on the same sites.*

*This photograph is characteristic : through the opening-up caused by demolition
can be seen two large buildings pushed apart, as it were, to receive a third
similar block. On this strategic spot between the Place de la Concorde and
the Opéra there will be a fragment of the New City and yet the antiquated
street will remain exactly the same !*

DESTRUCTIVE TO LIFE? FOR THE PROBLEM OF TRAFFIC IS
COMPLETELY IGNORED AND THE CREATION OF THESE COM-
MERCIAL ISLAND SITES AGGRAVATES THE DIFFICULTIES OF
TRANSIT. THESE PROFITABLE SPECULATIONS IN THE CENTRE
OF PARIS ARE LIKE THE NODES OF A CANCER WHICH HAVE
BEEN ALLOWED TO SETTLE ROUND THE HEART OF THE CITY,

AND WILL END BY STIFLING IT. TO ALLOW IT TO CONTINUE AS IT IS DOING IS AN ACT OF INCREDIBLE IRRESPONSIBILITY IN THE DANGEROUS PERIOD THROUGH WHICH ALL GREAT CITIES ARE PASSING.

I have put these lines in capitals because they proclaim a startling truth. Before we pronounce a final judgment let us analyze and consider the matter and then decide.

*

The Committee for the Preservation of Old Paris is hard at work.

It has been in existence for twenty-five years.

It is pleasant to think of a check on Vandalism. Everybody will agree, of course ! And it is comforting to read that Beauty is now ranked among the legitimate needs of the citizen.

And yet, harking back to my history lessons as a schoolboy, I call to mind those tragic moments when kings, emperors, and priests, seated in the midst of flowers, watched their exquisite slave girls dancing. But the gates of their city were forced, and the Barbarian rolled through like a flood, bringing carnage and death.

And here too, though the theme is simpler, it seems that we ought to look before us and not behind ; that there is a time for everything, and that the moment for pleasure is out of place if work has not preceded it.

*

If you are dying of heart disease or consumption you are not likely to spend time doing five-finger exercises on the piano.

Yet such words as Fatherland, Poetry, Ancestor worship, the Ideal are eloquent phrases flung about by numbers of people occupied in writing for the papers, whose mission is to direct public opinion. But when it comes to a question of demolishing rotten old houses full of tuberculosis and demoralizing, you hear them cry, " What about the iron-work, what about the beautiful old wrought-iron-work ? "

It may happen that the wife of one of these gentlemen has been doing a little " slumming " and has seen, and never forgotten, some delightful piece of iron-work in an old house which has now become a slum ; climbing some tottering old staircase on her errand of mercy. For these slums are haunted by relics of the past—of old France, of d'Artagnan, of the Précieuses. . . .

And so it comes to it that the phrase " One's Country " includes the perpetuation of these old staircases and all the degradation and misery of the slums.

Of course these lovers of the past who are so busy writing for the papers and directing public opinion will tell you, if you ask them, that they live in such-and-such a quarter, in a new building with lifts, etc., or in some wonderful little house hidden deep in a garden.

*

PHYSIC OR SURGERY

In 1923 the President of the Municipal Council of the City of Paris gave the first blow of the pickaxe to the immense mass of houses to be demolished to make way for the Boulevard Haussmann.

In 1925 the demolition had made great progress. The result was a large and impressive open space which brought many possibilities to one's mind. At that moment the space was there, not yet built over again, and the fact may well be considered one of great importance in the history of town planning, occurring as it did in the very heart of Paris. This bold piece of surgery must be credited to Haussmann, whose whole work had this character. When he began to cut Paris about so mercilessly, his contemporaries said it meant the end of the city. But modern motor traffic in Paris to-day is only possible thanks to Haussmann.

If we ask, therefore, whether such operations are possible or if the necessary steps of expropriation and indemnification are within the bounds of practical politics, we know that they *were* possible under Haussmann and the Emperor. And they are possible under our own democracy also.

This immense space which has been opened up in the jumbled and overcrowded city is deeply impressive. It is a proof.

SURGERY OR PHYSIC

The experience of the past answers : physic *and* the knife.
Surgery must be applied at the city's centre.
Physic must be used elsewhere.
We must use the knife to cope with that evolution which has passed through so many stages and has turned the ancient Lutetia into the Paris of to-day. Both the Middle Ages and the present day have inherited the same civic centre, which cannot

be moved to another position, since it is the hub of an immense wheel, the spokes of which run from great distances and have decided the point of their convergence. We shall only be in a position to use physic when able minds have foreseen and prepared for the future.

To-day we are deeply interested in the bringing about of a better future : one of its objects is to avoid these drastic operations. An immense and cheerful outer ring is being created : if the problem has been tackled in a large spirit, as it was in the days of Colbert, then it may prove a masterpiece of foresight. Are we taking the large point of view ? Or have æsthetics and poetry stolen a march on the modern factors of town planning, which may be reduced to the problem of traffic and that eternal necessity of the mind, ORDER.

Surgery is inevitable under present conditions.

Let us see what history has to teach us in this connection.

And first I must make this observation : no city of to-day has a *programme for dealing with traffic.* The problem is entirely new : it could not be foreseen fifty years ago. We are beset by the automatic effect of certain consequences. Till now it was the *fortified city* which constantly paralyzed town planning and kept us behind.

When the *Place Royale* was constructed (Place des Vosges) the four-wheeled coach was still unknown (Louis XIII).

In 1672 the Rue Galande was so narrow that it was impossible for two carriages to pass each other. Yet this street was part of the main network of arteries through Paris and served the bridges over the Seine.

About the middle of the sixteenth century there were only two coaches in Paris.

In 1658 there were 310.

In 1662 the first patent for public omnibuses was taken out.

In 1783 an edict was issued limiting for the first time the height of houses : the minimum width of the new streets was to be 30 feet (*this is a case of " physic "*).

During the Revolution an edict prescribed for five widths

of road : these were, roughly, 45 feet, 40 feet, 30 feet, 25 feet
and 20 feet ; no pavements were provided for (this is a case of
both *physic* and *surgery*).

Colbert was the initiator and creator of every important
reconstruction of Paris : buildings, boulevards, open spaces
and triumphal arches. The edict of 1676 was the first in the
world to enunciate a programme for public works adequate
for its own time and for the future (*physic* and *surgery*).

The general idea under Louis XIV was : " Paris is more
than a city : *it is a whole world.*" People were aware that new
developments were submerging old habits, and their efforts
were directed to legislating for the consequences. Even then
Paris was the first " Great City " of modern times ; it was ten
times less important than the Paris of to-day, yet only 200 years
lie between them.

In 1631 an edict attempted to limit the expansion of Paris
beyond the immediate suburbs—this expansion was incoherent
and not thought out. It was decided to erect thirty-one boundary posts to fix definitely the positions of the streets of the
suburbs and the extreme building limit ; beyond this it was
forbidden to build under penalty of confiscation and fines (this
was *physic*).

1724. In contradiction to this edict, "Malls " were planted
between these posts. Society began to move into these districts
and it was feared that the centre of the town would become
empty (*physic* again).

Napoleon I created the *Rue de Rivoli.* It was over 70 feet
wide, an extraordinary width for the period, for previously
to this streets had ranged from 45 to 20 feet in width (*surgery*).

1840. The boulevards begin, thanks to the foresight of
Colbert. An important event in the history of the life of the
city (*physic*).

1842. Railway stations. Saint-Lazare (*surgery*).

1847. The fortifications, the last walls to surround Paris,
and the protected zone of nearly 800 feet in depth (*physic*).

The sites for the stations were chosen in a somewhat

haphazard fashion. No one seems to have realized that they were the *new gates to the city*. There are no great avenues leading to them.

Later on it became necessary to open out new streets (*surgery*).

1853. Haussmann was nominated as " Préfet de la Seine."

The avenues he cut were entirely arbitrary : they were not based on strict deductions of the science of town planning. The measures he took were of a financial and military character (*surgery*).

Napoleon III built the *Avenue du Bois*, which was nearly 400 feet wide ; its length, in one straight line, was over 1400 yards (*physic*).

Streets little more than 20 feet wide are replaced by streets 75 feet and more in width (*surgery*).

Eighty-five miles of pavement become 775 : 40 miles of boulevards planted with trees become nearly 70. The number of trees lining them rises from 50,000 to 95,000.

One might quote examples indefinitely.

*

When Richelieu endowed Paris with a straight street nearly 30 feet wide and named it after himself he was accused of megalomania (*surgery*).

When Haussmann opened out the Boulevard Sébastopol he was accused of having created a desert in the very heart of Paris and of having made two separate cities of Paris (*surgery*).

A wide avenue with trees, cut by Le Nôtre through the woods on the rising ground which dominates the Tuileries from the west, brought to birth the possibilities of the future Champs Élysées, the glory of Paris of to-day and the only avenue which renders real services to motor traffic (the eighteenth-century engraving which shows this avenue right in the heart of the woods is very moving ; one cannot help reflecting that here we have the fruits of invention and fore-sight).

The plans of the eighteenth century reveal their makers as great designers.

In 1728 (*plan de l'Abbé*) many new "Malls," such as the Boulevard Montparnasse, were planted through existing market gardens. The network of streets was already there in the outer suburbs ; an arbitrary network since it grew up little by little upon the " Pack-Donkey's Way." But a few straight openings for streets, a sort of *vanguard*, were made, witnessing to human will and not mere chance : the Avenue de Vincennes and the Place du Trône, the Avenue de Saint Maur, the Fontaine-

LE NÔTRE'S CLEARING, SEEN FROM THE TUILERIES

bleau road through Villejuif, the Avenue de Saint-Denis, the Avenue de Neuilly which goes from the Tuileries to the Seine (over 3½ miles in length) ; the convergence of the avenues at the Étoile, where in each case 100 to 500 yards were marked out and planted in order to fix their directions. By 1731 the Bois de Boulogne is planned (on Roussel's plan) and the Parc de Montrouge. The Esplanade des Invalides is complete. One has a very real impression (looking at Robert de Vaugondy's map of 1760) of important works of reconstruction having been undertaken under the auspices of foreseeing administrators. These operations were immensely costly no

doubt. *But the work that was carried out on such broad lines
(i.e. on a geometrical basis) two centuries ago, through the midst
of market gardens, still provides the Paris of to-day with its vital
organs.*

By that date the Place Louis XV (Place de la Concorde)
was already built and the palaces were in course of construction. The corner of the Louvre becomes more and more of a
tangle. The great sewer is built. Everywhere roads spring
up in the form of lines as long and direct as possible (though
without much relation to each other). In 1763 the École
Militaire is built, and with the Champ de Mars stretches as far
as the Seine : the total area of the École would alone be able
to contain the Cité four or five times. In 1775 (J. B. Jaillot's
plan) new " Malls " are planted, later to become the Boulevard
Arago, the Lion de Belfort circus, Montparnasse, etc. The
Salpêtrière is built. The residential quarter has shifted : town
houses are now found in the Rue Saint-Dominique, the Rue de
Varennes, the Rue de l'Université, the Rue de Bourbon. In
1791 (Verniquet's plan) the Palais-Royal is rebuilt, the Louvre
surrounded by wretched hovels, the Place Vendôme blocked at
either end. The outer Boulevards have been built and planted ;
the Parc Monceau has been laid out on English lines, the Palais
Bourbon and its outbuildings have been constructed, and the
bridge of Louis XVI (Concorde).

Through all the eighteenth century we see this building and
rebuilding on a really impressive scale : the " Pack-Donkey's
Way," may still converge on the centre from the provinces, but
better ways are opposed to it. Clearings are put in hand,
cuttings through fields, gardens, woods and the suburban
clusters of houses. We have here at work an energetic surgery
whose results constitute the very framework of the gigantic
city, which the next century is to bring about. Paris in those
days had not 600,000 inhabitants ; yet men were even then
conceiving and carrying out the plans which have made possible
the city of the succeeding century with its four million inhabitants. The only great avenues for traffic were laid down by

Kings for their coaches ! [1]   It is a singular example of foresight
and energy and civic pride leading to action, and it saved the
city.   How, in the face of our timid tinkering and the misplaced
ingenuity of our pretty-pretty town planning, can the city of the

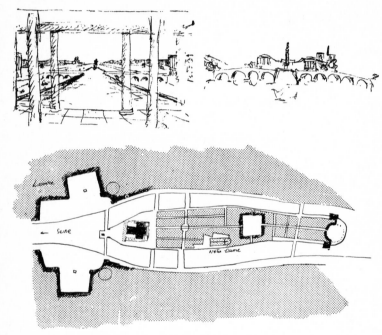

DRAWINGS SHOWING THE RADICAL TRANSFORMATION OF THE
" CITÉ "

*Notre Dame is the only thing left.   A single island was formed out of the
Cité and of the Île Saint-Louis.   Opposite the Pont Neuf a clearance was
made in order to provide a worthy continuation of the Colonnade of the Louvre.*

next century continue to live if it goes on growing at the present
rate ?

In that great age the question of remodelling the already
decayed centre of Paris was not lost sight of.   Great conferences took place whose object was to open up the city ; indeed

[1] At the height of the reign of Louis XIV there were in Paris not more than
310 coaches ; to-day there are 250,000 vehicles with a speed ten times greater.

to gut it and provide open spaces in the jumble of tiny streets. The Seine was taken as the axis for these attempts, since it was an open space. It was hoped to make an architectural monument of it, with its quays, its palaces, squares, monuments and fountains.

They cleared away. And this is *surgery*.

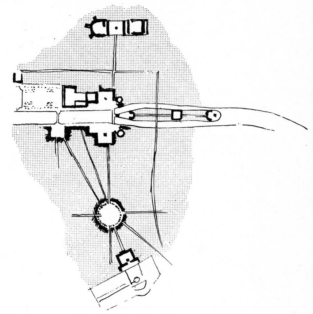

THE EIGHTEENTH CENTURY. REPLANNING OF THE QUARTERS ON AND AROUND THE SEINE
Straight streets are driven through the intolerable tangle.

This clearance went on over the whole surface of Paris in the *name of beauty*. The Circus de Tournon (160 yards in diameter), that of Bucy (150 yards in diameter), the demolition of Saint-Germain-l'Auxerrois (which resulted in an open square 180 yards by 130 yards), and so on.

A real need for a clearance led to all this removal of old buildings and consequently to open spaces, and long avenues and vistas ; and at the same time men had reached a point in regard to the æsthetics of architecture where corbellings and pointed gables were no longer tolerable ; they even went so far as to attack the cathedrals, so much did they dislike their barbaric and confused forms. This attitude arose almost in a moment as a result of a state of mind which had reached its highest form of expression in every department of thought (in Pascal, Voltaire, Rousseau, Mansart, Gabriel, Soufflot). In truth, under these absolute monarchs the full power of thought found expression and the Revolution was imminent : here again we have surgery.

Past history provides us with innumerable and forceful examples. Foresight and control are essential : physic and surgery. And always there must be clearsightedness and decision.

The Paris of to-day, practically speaking, no longer has any horses, but instead of these we have 250,000 vehicles running at speeds ten times greater which fill the streets. We owe great thanks to Colbert and to the Le Roys for having prepared, in their own calmer days, these avenues which to-day form our sole arterial system.

Now that we have the motor-car, the airplane, and the railway, would it not seem a sort of mental cowardice to go on being satisfied with the sumptuous but decayed heritage of the past ?

The franc to-day is worth about 2*d*. The urban splendours inherited by us are like the depreciated franc : the motor has reduced their value in the proportion of 10 to 1, while population has increased tenfold : our heritage does not seem worth very much in face of our needs.

Yet it seems to be all that we can have, so long as we are content to be æsthetes harping on the beauty of old cottages in rural settings. We refuse to recognize the thing which is advancing upon us. There is no physic (*i.e.* foresight) nor surgery (*i.e.* decision). The city will soon reach a stage of deadlock, since all that people care about are trifling improvements. Yet the city's heart and lungs are mortally sick.

Haussmann came after Louis XIV, Louis XV, Louis XVI, and Napoleon I. His demolitions were carried out remorselessly in the very centre of Paris, and of a Paris intolerable to any person capable of thought. It may be said in general that the more Haussmann rebuilt, the more money he made ; he reshaped large portions of Paris and thereby filled the coffers of his Emperor. And all that was done by this man, who turned a deaf ear to the clamours with which he was assailed on every hand, was to replace sordid six-storeyed buildings by sumptuous six-storeyed buildings and to turn noisome and infected parts of the city into magnificent ones. Had he tried to create boulevards on the outskirts he would have ruined himself. It was just because his operations were confined to the very centre itself that they proved profitable.

And fifty years after this money-making surgery you have the spectacle of a Paris which would have been unable to exist or to continue its vital system but for the fact that Haussmann and a few other determined men before him had already largely reshaped it, and with admirable foresight had given the city a powerful dose of medicine.

Picture to yourself one of those immense *battues*, where hundreds of thousands of rabbits are frightened into a series of traps formed of narrow corridors in which they get wedged and are caught. But in this infernal machine there are some much wider passages through which the rabbits may flee without getting stuck—that is, not immediately. All the rabbits pour into the wide passages in a mad rush.

The great city is such a trap and the motors in it are the rabbits. The wide passages are those built by Colbert, Napoleon I or Haussmann. But none the less, in the end, the rabbits get stuck.

To conclude. Up till 1900 no one had any idea, even the faintest notion, of the phenomenon about to burst on the world. First came the motor-car ; then the airplane. The railroads had already caused a certain disturbance, but humanity was fully occupied in providing for the needs of the age. But to-day,

THE RUE DE RIVOLI FORMED AND THE LOUVRE OPENED OUT.

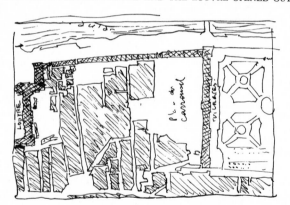

THE LOUVRE OPENED OUT.

THE BRIDGES WERE SWEPT CLEAR OF THEIR HOUSES.

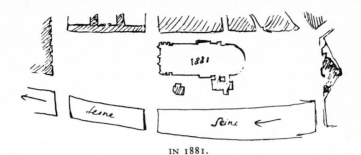

IN 1881.

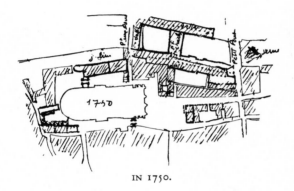

IN 1750.

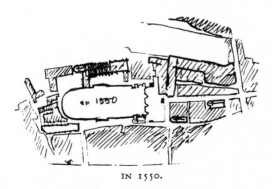

IN 1550.

NOTRE-DAME OPENED OUT; ALL THE BUILDINGS ON THE ISLAND
PULLED DOWN AND REBUILT.

in the very midst of a mechanical age, an age of speed, we are still absorbed in the problem of forming new suburbs with winding avenues pleasant to walk about in. And in the city the competent authorities are demanding a reduction in the authorized height of buidings. . . .

And all the time the universal use of machinery continues to produce its consequences.

*

SURGERY

In February 1925 I was on the jury of the international competition for the extension of the city of Strasbourg. Various plans were submitted to us for making use of the acquired sites (roads of approach, adjoining villages, etc.), all of which suggested enlarging those existing elements, which admittedly were definitely conditioned by chance. This is indeed one of the popular theories of modern town planning and a practice widely spread : *i.e.* rearranging, tinkering.

"Common-sense" accepts such conceptions very easily: they look businesslike, they have an air of being true and reasonable and not to be denied. The active, healthy and practical mind that deals with realities is sympathetic to them.

We also had before us some extremely daring projects, but of the kind that are called "dangerous," "Utopian," "unrealizable"—not of this earth. . . . They amused us for a moment or two, for we saw as in a mirage or a dream a Promised Land we should never reach. Our active, healthy and practical minds wasted very little time on such schemes and turned resolutely away.

After a first morning spent in a general examination of the various projects, the jury was taken by car to the surrounding countryside along roads which ran through cultivated fields and forests, and through villages which are, as it were, the outposts of the city.

My companion represented the Chamber of Commerce of

Strasbourg on the jury. He was quite naturally in favour of any opportune scheme. In going through the main streets of villages I said, " Do you see how you have to slow up when the road winds ? " On the stretches of straight road running through forest he " stepped " on the accelerator and seemed

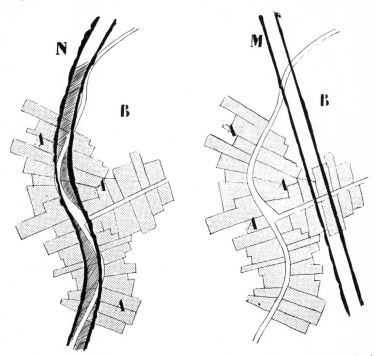

In this diagram all the proprietors take undue advantage of being bought out and the road still remains a winding one.

In this practically no one is interfered with and the road becomes straight.

delighted. But when the road wound about on the level, he slowed down and went carefully. " These winding roads are a great nuisance ! " I asked him to stop in the middle of a bridge over the canal constructed by Napoleon I. " This canal goes in an absolutely straight line right across the country. The straight line is deeply impressive in the confusion of nature ;

it is the *work of men*. It is inspiring and even poetical in the midst of this nondescript landscape." Further on : " Look at the railway ; it goes straight on, always straight on, conscious of its job ; it is a witness to human will—a *positive* thing." Further on : " This port is a work of *order*. It is beautiful ! Let us be silent a moment—the port is a work of order because it solves a problem which has been clearly realized."

We were going through Neudorf (an important centre to the south of Strasbourg). " You see," he said, "all we have to do in this case is to widen the main street and straighten out the curve a little. It would be economical and satisfactory." " Well," I said, " as you have slowed down a good deal, let us look round a little. If you widen out one side only to save expense, even then all the proprietors on that side of the road will have to be compensated, and as they know they are on an important road of the future they will ask a lot. Even if you were to cut straight through the curving street the cost would be the same. But now look at the level ground behind those houses ; form a straight avenue *there* and your compensation will be limited to that for ordinary agricultural land." But an architect who was present interjected : " Your straight avenue would seem interminable, one would die of boredom on it." I was astounded and replied, " You have a car and yet you say that ! If you think for one moment you will realize that it is a question of linking up the future great business centre with the future great port ; it is essential, therefore, that motors can travel as directly as possible." When we again took up our work of examining the various schemes my companion, who had been totally shaken in his stereotyped convictions (realistic, practical and common-sense ideas, as people say), was a new man. Little by little, as the work of the jury progressed, we felt that our part in the affair became more important, and certainly more serious than those who had invited us could have imagined. " Think," I would often say to my colleagues during our sessions, " that fifty years from now our work will be quoted : people will say, ' Men came from Paris to *determine*, and that during a conference which only lasted a few days, *the fate of Strasbourg and the future life of the city of Strasbourg.'* We can perform our task either extremely well or extremely badly. What will the motor-car be in fifty years ? We cannot agree to a merely *convenient* solution, we cannot betray the straight line. Imagine these winding roads enlarged for the car of fifty years hence ; the winding road which is still the *Pack-Donkey's Way*. If we must cut wider roads, let us do so, but only through some farm building or unimportant suburb. Napoleon traced out the straight canal because his instinct was towards *order :* engineers constructed the docks of the port geometrically because mankind expresses itself thus. Haussmann traced his rectilinear Boulevards because he was a practical man devoid of poetical feeling. Louis XV and Louis XVI traced their rectilinear Boulevards because they were æsthetes and were anxious that the record of their reigns should be manifest in the grandeur of their enterprises. Vauban traced his geometrical bastions because he was a military man. . . ."

Organization involves a geometrical plan : to create geometrically, whether in the midst of nature or of the magma which has resulted " naturally " from the grouping of men in urban crowds, surgery must be employed.

" You trace out straight lines, fill up the holes and level up the ground, and the result is nihilism. . . ." (*Sic.*)

(From an angry speech of a great authority who was presiding on a Commission to report on plans for extension.)

I replied :

" Excuse me, but that, properly speaking, is just what our work should be."

(This incident is authentic.)

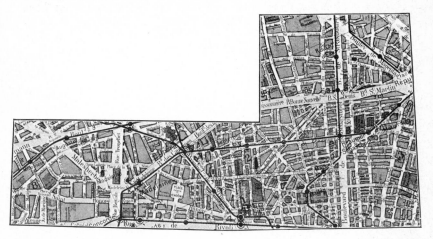

THE PART OF PARIS AFFECTED BY THE "VOISIN" PLAN

XV

THE CENTRE OF PARIS

THE "Voisin Plan" [1] for Paris is the result of combining two new essential elements : *a commercial city* and *a residential city*.

The *commercial city* would occupy 600 acres of a particularly antiquated and unhealthy part of Paris, *i.e.* from the Place

---

[1] As it is the motor-car which has completely overturned all our old ideas of town planning, I thought of interesting the manufacturers of cars in the construction of the *Esprit Nouveau* Pavilion at the Paris International Exhibition of Decorative Art, since this Pavilion was planned as a dwelling and as a unit of modern town planning.

I saw the heads of the Peugeot, Citroën and Voisin Companies and said to them :
" The motor has killed the great city.
" The motor must save the great city.
" Will you endow Paris with a Peugeot, Citroën or Voisin scheme of rebuilding; a scheme whose sole object would be to concentrate public notice on the true architectural problem of this era, a problem not of decoration but of architecture and town

THE " TOWN-PLANNING " STAND OF THE ESPRIT NOUVEAU AT THE
EXHIBITION OF DECORATIVE ART AT PARIS, 1925

*In the background can be seen the " Voisin" plan for Paris and various
diagrams dealing with traffic problems, housing schemes, new types of
buildings, and so on. On the right is the Panorama of a " Contemporary
City of 3,000,000 inhabitants," and on the left the Panorama of the " Voisin"
plan. These painted diagrams are on canvases measuring over 80 square
yards and over 60 square yards respectively.*

de la République to the Rue du Louvre, and from the Gare de
l'Est to the Rue de Rivoli.

The *residential city* would extend from the Rue des Pyramides to the circus on the Champs Élysées, and from the Gare
Saint-Lazare to the Rue de Rivoli, and would involve the destruction of areas which for the most part are overcrowded, and
covered with middle-class houses now used as offices.

---

planning; a sane reconstruction of the dwelling unit and the creation of urban
organs which would answer to our conditions of living which have been so profoundly affected by machinery ? "

Messrs. Peugeot would not risk themselves on our venturesome scheme.

M. Citroën very amiably replied that he did not know what I was talking about,
and did not see what the motor-car had to do with the problem of the centre of Paris.

M. Mongermon, of the Voisin Company, without any hesitation agreed to
finance my researches into the question of the centre of Paris, and so the resulting
scheme is called the " Voisin " scheme for Paris.

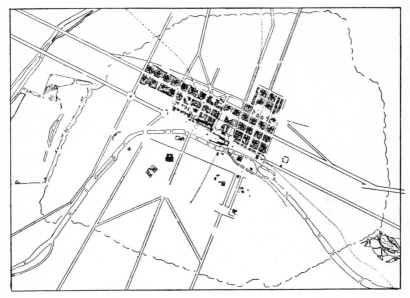

THE FIRST SKETCH PLAN OF THE SCHEME FOR REARRANGING THE
CENTRE OF PARIS

The central station would be between the business city and the residential city, and would be underground.

The principal axis of the new plan of the centre of Paris would lie east to west, from Vincennes to Levallois-Perret. It would recreate one of the indispensable great transversal arteries which no longer exist to-day. It would serve as the principal artery for fast traffic ; it would be nearly 400 feet wide, and would have a speedway for one-way traffic without cross roads. The effect of this vital artery would be to empty the Champs Élysées, which quite clearly cannot continue to serve as a main thoroughfare for fast traffic, since it ends in a blank wall : *i.e.* at the Jardin des Tuileries.[1]

[1] The recent proposal to continue the Champs Élysées through the Tuileries, as far as to where the Rue des Tuileries crosses, is nonsense, since the latter street runs at one end into the Rue de Rivoli and the Rue des Pyramides, both of which are already crowded beyond their capacity, and, at the other end, into the Pont Royal, which is a complete bottle-neck. The Pont Royal feeds the Rue du Bac, which is only about 40 feet wide and in which all traffic has to be one-way. Who is responsible for such mad ideas ?

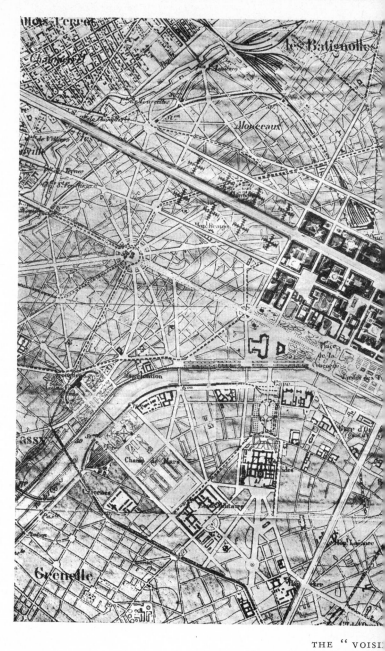

THE "VOISI
(*Shown in the Pavilion of the Esprit Nouvea*

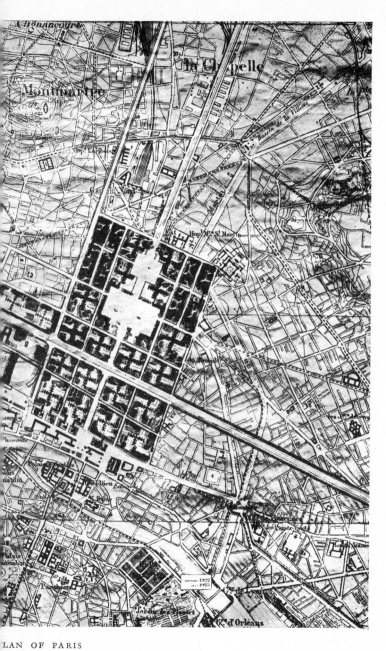

LAN OF PARIS

(*e Exhibition of Decorative Art, Paris,* 1925.)

The " Voisin " scheme for Paris means regaining possession of the eternal centre of the city. I showed in a former chapter how it was impossible in practice to displace the settled centres of great cities and to create an adequate new city at the side of the old one.[1]

This plan makes a frontal attack on the most diseased quarters of the city, and the narrowest streets : it is not " opportunist " or designed to gain a yard or two at odd points in over-congested roads. Its aim is rather to open up in the strategic heart of Paris a splendid system of communication. As against streets ranging from 20 to 35 feet in width with cross roads

1925.   SKETCH FOR THE " CENTRE OF PARIS "

every 20, 30 or 50 yards, its aim is to establish a plan on the " gridiron " system with roads 150, 250 to 400 feet in width, with cross roads every 350 or 400 yards ; and on the vast island sites thus formed to build immense cruciform sky-scrapers, so creating a *vertical* city, a city which will pile up the cells which have for so long been crushed on the ground, and set them high above the earth, bathed in light and air.

Thenceforward, instead of a flattened-out and jumbled city such as *the airplane reveals to us for the first time*, terrifying in its confusion (see the plates), our city rises vertical to the sky, open to light and air, clear and radiant and sparkling. The soil, of whose surface 70 to 80 per cent. has till now been

[1] It is true that during the Renaissance new cities were constructed contiguous to an old one.   The reason was entirely military, and the ancient city being extremely small there would have been no gain in rebuilding the centre.

encumbered by closely packed houses, is now built over to the extent of a mere 5 per cent. The remaining 95 per cent. is devoted to the main speedways, car parks and open spaces. The avenues of trees are doubled and quadrupled, and the parks at the foot of the sky-scrapers do, in fact, make the city itself one vast garden.

The density, which is too great as things are at present, of the districts affected by the " Voisin " plan would not be reduced. It would be *quadrupled*.

Instead of those terrible districts with which we are so little acquainted,[1] which have a density of population of 320 to the acre, these new quarters would allow of 1,400 to the same area.

I wish it were possible for the reader, by an effort of imagination, to conceive what such a vertical city would be like ; imagine all this junk, which till now has lain spread out over the soil like a dry crust, cleaned off and carted away and replaced by immense clear crystals of glass, rising to a height of over 600 feet ; each at a good distance from the next and all standing with their bases set among trees. Our city, which has crawled on the ground till now, suddenly rises to its feet in the most natural way, even for the moment going beyond the powers of our imaginations, which have been constrained by age-long habits of thought.

For the Pavilion of the *Esprit Nouveau* at the International Exhibition of Decorative Art held in Paris, and in which the " Voisin " plan was on view, I painted a panorama whose aim was to make evident *to the eye* this new conception, so unfamilar to us as yet. The panorama was most carefully executed and showed Paris as it is to-day, from Notre-Dame to the Étoile, including those monuments which are our imperishable heritage. Behind it rose the new city. But one is no longer confronted with the spires and campaniles of a wild Manhattan,

---

[1] I should like any of my readers who may find themselves able to do so to take a walk in the daytime, and another at night, in the districts of Paris covered by the " Voisin " plan. They would be surprised !

PANORAMA OF T**

(Shown in the Pavilion of the Esprit Nouveau

jostling against one another and mutually robbing each other of light and air, but the majestic rhythm of vertical surfaces receding into the distance in a noble perspective and outlining pure forms. From one sky-scraper to another a relationship of voids and solids is established. At their feet the great open spaces are seen. The city is once more based on axes, as is every true architectural creation. Town planning enters into architecture and architecture into town planning. If the " Voisin " plan is studied there can be seen to west and south-west the great openings made by Louis XIV, Louis XV and Napoleon : the Invalides, the Tuileries, the Place de la Con-corde, the Champ de Mars and the Étoile. These works are a signal example of *creation*, of that spirit which is able to dominate aud compel the mob. Set in juxtaposition the new *business city* does not seem an anomaly, but rather gives the

VOISIN " SCHEME FOR PARIS

Exhibition of Decorative Art, Paris, 1925.)

impression of being in the same tradition and following the
normal laws of progress.

Business, which since the War has been on the lookout for
offices, is practically unable to find them. And so the office
buildings I have already denounced are gradually being erected.
An office is a definite organ which has nothing in common
with a dwelling. The working day demands a type of building
which we may call an " implement for toil." The business city
of the " Voisin " scheme offers a definite suggestion, carefully
worked out and quite feasible, for housing what may be termed
the G.H.Q. of Business. By a logical series of inferences it is
clear that Paris, which is the capital of France, must in this
twentieth century construct its Business General Headquarters.
It would seem, therefore, that our analysis has led us to formulate
a reasonable proposition. Each sky-scraper is able to house

These houses are on an average seven storeys high.
Is this a picture of the seventh circle of Dante's Inferno?   Alas, no !   It shows the terrible conditions under which hundreds of thousands of people have to live.   The city of Paris does not possess these denunciatory photographic documents.   This general bird's-eye view is like a blow between the eyes.   In our walks through this maze of streets we are enraptured by their picturesque-ness, so redolent of the past.   But tuberculosis, demoralization, misery and shame are doing the devil's work among them.   As for the " Committee of Old Paris," it is busy collecting antiques.

This view from the air of the Champs Élysées district is incomparably
superior to that on the left. But both are the result of drift and opportunism.
It is a dreadful thing to look at these old realities which are so shocking to the
spirit of to-day.

from 20,000 to 40,000 employees. Thus the eighteen sky-scrapers shown would contain 500,000 to 700,000 people, the army engaged in the direction of business.

The tube railways pass under and serve each sky-scraper ; the roads and the motor tracks provide what is needed to enable this enormous crowd to circulate freely.

The railway lines of the Gare de l'Est are covered over by a concrete roadway with a superimposed motor track. This new main artery leading north is built upon more or less undeveloped land.

A cross road leading south could start from the new central station between the residential city and the business city.

The great artery running *east to west*, which is to-day totally lacking, would act as a channel into which would pour the traffic which is bottled up in the shapeless network of streets of to-day. This great artery would deliver us from the present street system, so shut in upon itself, and would open up a way into the country at its two extremities.

The residential city which is situated to the west of the new Central Station would bring to the centre of Paris a series of magnificently airy quarters, with Government offices rising to a height of 100 to 120 feet. The Ministries would be regrouped. There would be halls and buildings for every purpose ; and lastly the great hotels.

The Central Station would be a considerable improvement on the scheme I suggested in 1922, where the main lines came to a dead end. In this scheme all the lines run through on a loop system. To east, west, north and south there would be four great stations, or rather platforms, where passengers could be taken up or set down ; the trains would thus always be *through* trains, never at a prolonged standstill, never in process of being made up. They arrive all ready, take up their load and go off, always as " one-way " traffic.

*

THE " VOISIN " SCHEME AND THE PAST

In this scheme the historical past, our common inheritance, is respected. More than that, it is *rescued*. The persistence of the present state of crisis must otherwise lead rapidly to the destruction of that past.

First of all I must make a distinction, of a sentimental nature, but one of great importance ; in these days the past has lost something of its fragrance, for its enforced mingling with the life of to-day has set it in a false environment. My dream is to see the Place de la Concorde empty once more, silent and lonely, and the Champs Élysées a quiet place to walk in. The " Voisin " scheme would isolate the whole of the ancient city and bring back peace and calm from Saint-Gervais to the Étoile.

The districts of the *Marais*, the *Archives*, the *Temple*, etc., would be demolished. But the ancient churches would be preserved.[1] They would stand surrounded by verdure ; what could be more charming ! And even if we must admit that their original environment has thus been transformed, we must agree that their present setting is not only an unreal one, but is also dreary and ugly.

Similarly the " Voisin " plan shows, still standing among the masses of foliage of the new parks, certain historical monuments, arcades, doorways, carefully preserved because they are pages out of history or works of art.

Thus one might find, surrounded by green grass, an exciting and delightful relic such as, say, some fine Renaissance house, now to be used as a library, lecture hall or what not.

The " Voisin " scheme covers 5 per cent. only of the ground with buildings, it safeguards the relics of the past and enshrines them harmoniously in a framework of trees and woods. For material things too must die, and these green parks with their relics are in some sort cemeteries, carefully tended, in which people may breathe, dream and learn. In this way the past

[1] This was not one of the objects of the plan, but was merely the result of their falling into the architectural composition of the scheme.

becomes no longer dangerous to life, but finds instead its true place within it.

The " Voisin " scheme does not claim to have found a final solution to the problem of the centre of Paris ; but it may serve to raise the discussion to a level in keeping with the spirit of our age, and to provide us with reasonable standards by which to judge the problem. It sets up *principles* as against the medley of silly little reforms with which we are constantly deceiving ourselves.

AMERICA

Here is the exact opposite of what the " Voisin " scheme proposes for Paris

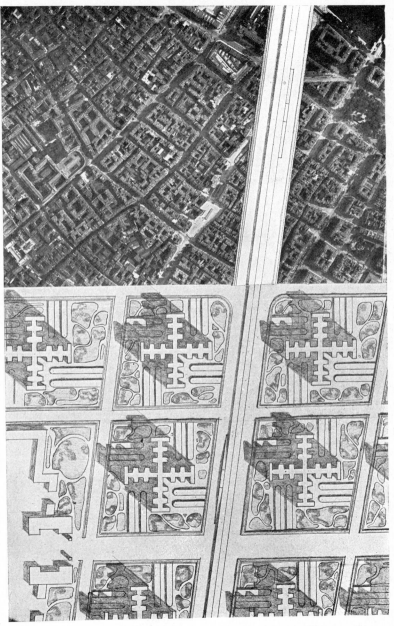

Here is the solution proposed by the "Voisin" Scheme. Here are the districts which it is proposed to demolish and those which it is suggested should be built in their place. Both plans are to the same scale.

" But where is the money coming from ? "

A stereotyped question—first raised in 1922.

PARIS ATTEND DE L'ÉPOQUE :
LE SAUVETAGE DE SA VIE MENACÉE
LA SAUVEGARDE DE SON BEAU PASSÉ
LA MANIFESTATION MAGNIFIQUE ET
PUISSANTE DE L'ESPRIT DU XX° SIÈCLE

Des quartiers entiers ne sont plus que de la pourriture, des foyers de maladie, de tristesse, de démoralisation. Une grande
opération financière semblable sur une échelle infiniment plus vaste, à celle d'Haussmann, apporterait à la ville des bénéfices
financiers énormes (se souvenir qu'Haussmann construisit des maisons à six étages à la place de maisons de six étages,
et qu'aujourd'hui, on peut construire des maisons de soixante ou de douze étages à la place de maisons de six étages).

THE MANIFESTO USED IN CONNECTION WITH THE PANORAMA AT THE
SALON D'AUTOMNE, 1922

XVI

FINANCE AND REALIZATION

WHEN I began to write this book, I thought I would
entrust some well-known economist with this chapter on
the financial aspect, so that my architectural conclusions might
be ratified indisputably by figures. But daily preoccupations
and the general rush of existence carried me on from one day
to another without any time for collecting the necessary information. Finally, it was too late, so this chapter on Figures
must be without them !

These were the points I wished to put to my economist.

(*a*) First of all, work out the ground values of the properties affected by my scheme ; then figure out the cost of demolition, of reconstruction and of the improvement of the said sites
and the new value of the new quarters when built ; and then,
subtracting one set of figures from the other, calculate the profit
that would result.

(*b*) Draw up an estimate of the number of firms likely to
become tenant-owners of offices in the new blocks. Calculate
the sum that could be raised privately to such an end. Arrange
for the deficiency to be provided by a public issue. It is better
that this immense undertaking on behalf of the public should
be financed by the public and not by the State (which would

not be using it). Find out where and in what country the necessary money could best be raised, and on the best terms.

(c) Given the immense sums needed, calculate the effect upon the French currency of these holdings by foreigners in connection with such an important part of the soil of Paris and its buildings.

But as I am reduced to setting forth myself the financial side of my scheme, I will do in a rough-and-ready way what my economist's analysis and calculations would have done in detail. I shall treat the question from the simple common-sense point of view ; thus we shall get some definite direction. After all, is that not the way things go in this world ? Everybody, in his own special domain, is willing to undertake the solution of the most delicate and complicated problems ; but to start him off there must always be some flash of thought, which must be true in a general sense, and of general significance. It is always some such " idea " that leads a man to persevere in the search for a solution in a direction thus predetermined.

To suggest the demolition and reconstruction of the centre of Paris may seem to many a joke in rather bad taste. But if a succession of considerations has shown, again and again, *from many angles and many points of view*, that such action is inevitable, what does that mean ? Does it not mean that we must, first of all, remodel the centre of the city and build vertically ?

Now follow " Finance " and " Realization."

The centres of great cities represent the most important of all land values. Let us call this value A. Haussmann pulled down the crumbling districts of Paris and replaced them by sumptuous quarters. His efforts were really financial operations and he filled the Emperor's coffers with gold. To the value A he gave a value five times greater, which we may call 5A.

But Haussmann merely replaced old and decayed buildings of six storeys by fine new buildings of six storeys. Therefore the revaluation he brought about was due to *quality*, not to quantity.

But if, while following his example, we also increased the density of population from 300 to 1,300 inhabitants per acre, we should quadruple the capacity of the new districts so that their land value would be not 5A, but four times this : $4 \times 5A$.

The moral is that we must not say, " But . . . what immense sums would have to be *sunk* in all this expropriation and reconstruction," but rather, "*What an opportunity for capital for almost incredible amounts would be created by such an attempt at revaluation!*"

And this revaluation is possible, but the *first and essential condition* is that there should be a large and noble scheme for the improvement of the centre of Paris.

Any economist, when inquiring into the financial basis of this scheme, would seek to determine what the profits would be in relation to the admittedly great cost of such operations. When once that has been established, the matter becomes of importance to the Government.

The *Minister of Finance could find immense financial resources in the very centre of Paris.*

Such a project could never lead to private speculation of an undesirable character for very good reasons.

If a decree were passed for the general expropriation of the centre of Paris, the value of the land would stand at a certain figure which we will call A. This figure can easily be ascertained by experts from the contemporary records of sales of land at various points in Paris. The value is thus A. The construction of a " Business City " at once raises this value A to 5A, and the increase in density would make this $4 \times 5A$. Thus there is a new value, twenty times the original value, A, out of which compensation can be paid. And even if we reckon this new value at the lowest possible figure, it is still obvious that the margin is so great that compensation could be paid at the highest market price ; and the process of expropriation could thus be effected without delay and at an equitable rate.

We have only to erect our sixty-storey buildings and this new and immense wealth is at our disposal.

*

Who is to pay for the building of these immense business blocks ? The *Users* of them. There are legions in Paris who would gladly give up the middle-class flats in the various quarters of Paris in which they have to carry on their businesses and would take over, as tenant-owners, each their appropriate floor-space in a sky-scraper. The users would be the proprietors of the sky-scraper.

There are, of course, others who are running " young " businesses or who for various reasons would be unable to buy space in the sky-scraper ; these firms would rent their floor-space from those who had the available capital to buy it.

And what about the others ? A part of the necessary financial resources is already in the country : a great part is elsewhere. Are we then to invite foreigners to take a share in the enterprise ? Are we to offer the centre of Paris, with its noble sites and buildings, our national riches and splendour to Americans, English, Japanese or Germans ?

Yes, certainly.

It would be a good thing if part of the centre of Paris belonged to foreigners. It would be a good thing for millions of international capital to be employed in raising these gigantic towers of glass in the centre of Paris, and for a part of this centre to belong to Americans or Germans ; for would they not then take good care that it was not destroyed by long-range guns or bombing airplanes ?

So perhaps there may lie a remedy against War in the Air in the internationalization of the centre of Paris. America would not permit its destruction, Germany would take good care not to harm it ! We all know that great wars are created by the great capitals.

If twenty sky-scrapers over 500 feet in length and 600 feet in height were set thus in the centre of Paris, Paris would be protected from all barbarian destruction.

That should mean something to the War Office.

*

It is no longer possible, as in Haussmann's day, to throw whole districts into confusion, drive out the tenants, and make a desert in the crowded heart of Paris over a space of three or even five years. The housing question is too critical for such a procedure to be possible.

In my scheme, sky-scrapers accommodating 40,000 employees take up 5 per cent. of the available site. Thus actually only 5 per cent. of the population would be dislodged in the re-building. Therefore the project is a feasible one, since it is also a measure of public utility (as for those urban troglodytes, the 5 per cent. of the inhabitants of the Marais, the Archives, and the Temple districts, they could be transferred to the garden cities and our enhanced resources would even allow us to *present* them with free cottages).

The completed sky-scraper would only take up 5 per cent. of the available site, and during building operations it would take up no more space. Constructed of steel and glass it would contain no stone, and therefore it would not be necessary to cart masses of building stone from the country into the heart of the city ; and the sky-scraper would rise easily and gently upon its foundations, with its bolts and rivets. It would really be a factory production, and made in a steel-yard near Paris, or even away in the country.

At the end of three years, or it may be five, the sky-scraper is completed. Then the process of moving begins. From various districts the new tenants throng in : old office suites are emptied and others move into them, leaving their own apartments free, and so on. In this way the district round the sky-scraper is cleared. It is demolished, avenues are cut through it and the parks and plantations laid out.

The Minister for Public Works could reconstitute the centre of Paris without injuring a single individual.

*

.   .   .   .

My rôle has been a technical one. I have attempted to fill it as conscientiously as I could by a close study of the *cell* (which is the necessary and sufficient housing unit), and of the consequences arising out of its collective grouping ; the while I sought to discover exactly how the development of a city takes place and to find a formula which should give the rules for classification on which all modern town planning must rest. I had a good acquaintance with the technical equipment at our disposal, and my inquiry having led me to an understanding of the way in which a city must develop, I was able to work out, untrammelled by minor considerations, a scheme for the re-planning of the centre of a Great City. At the same time I took care not to outrage legitimate susceptibilities ; and to that end I respected, and indeed took care to protect, the memorials of our older culture.

My scheme is brutal, because town existence and life itself are brutal : life is pitiless, it must defend itself, hemmed in as it is on all sides by death. To overcome death, constant activity is necessary.

I have suggested, and on a plane infinitely above the losing fight in which the public authorities are continually engaged, a scheme which is really a *scheme*, *i.e.* a programme and a creation of the mind, an insistent challenge to inertia and to preoccupation with unimportant special cases. My position is that a society which is on a mechanical basis has replaced an older society whose equilibrium had remained constant through the centuries. Machinery has projected us into a new epoch ; yet none the less we still find ourselves in full occupation of the same civic organ—the city—and in the same spot where, for very good reasons, the city grew up and must *remain*. I invent no *Utopia* in which to build my city. I assert that its proper place is *here*, and nothing will remove it. If I affirm this so categorically it is because I am aware of our human limitations, aware that we have not the power to begin all over again and build our City as we will elsewhere. To desire such a thing is to be reactionary, and to persist in it would make the whole scheme an impossibility. Therefore it must be *here*.

The project so often mooted, of displacing the centre of Paris and removing it to Saint-Germain-en-Laye or to the plain of Saint-Denis, is, as I have demonstrated, not technically possible. Financially such a move would cause a terrible catastrophe, owing to the fall in the value of the *centre*, which in itself represents a large proportion of the national wealth. In the old centre, values representing many millions would, by a stroke of the pen, be reduced to nothing ; and on the new site many millions would be swallowed up in the building of the new city.

By an arbitrary and illegitimate process a site at present worth almost nothing would become immensely valuable, whilst the immense riches of the existing site would be annihilated. Such an injustice, and such a technical impossibility, cannot prevail against reason.

In this book I have sought for fundamental bases, since discussions of this kind generally tend to wander away from vital and objective considerations and to lose themselves and founder in a philosophical morass. It is for this reason that I have insisted on *Order* as being the key to every action, and *Sensibility* as the directing force of every impulse.

My book is lacking in figures, and it is a great pity. Someone else, a specialist, will, I hope, go into them now the problem has been put forward. Figures are all-important, I know. But they are sometimes + and sometimes —. In this case I am convinced they are +. I am certain also that the time is very near, for sooner or later everything comes to maturity. Modern town planning must be accepted. If we do not recognize this, what is there left for us to do ? To mark time ? But this is impossible. We have reached a turning-point, and if we hold back, man with his fundamental egotism will take action to his own selfish advantage, and the new city will be rebuilt on the old sites, as is already being done. We shall be stifled in this so-called " new " city ; the great city will fall into decay and gradually it will disappear from history.

Those who are closely in touch with the Administrative Departments concerned, whose hasty decisions have to be made from day to day, are necessarily too much affected by special cases. They are in the thick of the fight, and it is impossible for them to take a broad view. I am in a position of detachment and a free-lance, and I mean to remain so. It pleased me to carry my reasoning as far as was analytically possible, as far indeed as was permitted by pure theory, and it is theory that has led me to certain definite conclusions.

These conclusions are brief and summary, and are put forward without the necessary qualifications which should be made. But their trend is entirely practical, and above all they have brought the discussion back on to a healthy plane.

I do not feel I am breaking with tradition : I believe myself to be absolutely traditional in my theories. All the great works of the past, one after another, confirm my statement that the essential spirit of any period is bound to have an equivalent in material things.

And there is one consideration which gives this work a right to appear before the public ; it is that the matter is urgent.

*

People tax me very readily with being a revolutionary. It is an effective if somewhat flattering way of putting a distance between a society preoccupied with maintaining its present equilibrium and eager minds which are likely to disturb it. Yet this equilibrium which they try so hard to maintain is for vital reasons purely ephemeral : it is a balance which has to be perpetually re-established.

On the other hand, since the Russian Revolution it has become the charming prerogative of both our own and the

Bolshevist revolutionaries to keep the title of revolutionary to themselves alone. Everything which has not chosen ostensibly to adopt their label they call bourgeois and capitalist and stupid.

It was inevitable that the scheme for town planning which I exhibited at the Salon d'Automne of 1922 should be the occasion of a number of articles in Communist organs. One part of my scheme—the technical side—was praised, but the rest was severely criticized because I had not labelled the finest buildings on my plan " People's Hall," " Soviet," or " Syndical-ist Hall," and so on; and because I did not crown my plan with the slogan " Nationalization of all property."

I have been very careful not to depart from the technical side of my problem. I am an architect; no one is going to make a politician of me. Everyone, in his own domain where he is an expert, can apply his special knowledge and carry his solutions to their logical conclusion. On my plans, I write, " Administrative Services," " Public Services," etc., and that is quite sufficient. In my scheme for the centre of Paris I have mentioned a " Measure for the General Expropriation of the Centre of the City," and I claim that under my scheme it will be possible to compensate owners up to the full *present* value of their property, as this will have risen so enormously in value. So that there need be no injury or spoliation, nor is the ruin of any landowner, large or small, involved.

Economic and social progress can only be the result of technical problems which have found a proper solution.

The aim of this work has been the unfolding of a clear solution ; its value depends on its success in that direction. It has no label, it is not dedicated to our existing Bourgeois-Capitalist Society nor to the Third International. It is a technical work.

And I do not propose to bear witness in the highways and byways as though I belonged to the Salvation Army.

Things are not revolutionized by making revolutions. The real Revolution lies in the solution of existing problems.

LOUIS XIV COMMANDING THE BUILDING OF THE INVALIDES

Homage to a great town planner.

This despot conceived immense projects and realized them. Over all the country his noble works still fill us with admiration. He was capable of saying, " We wish it," or " Such is our pleasure."